Selected and edited by Abi May
Cover design: Gentian Suçi
Design: M-A Mignot based on a design
    by Gentian Suçi
ISBN: 978-3-03730-703-8

© Aurora Production AG, Switzerland, 2012
Printed in Taiwan.

www.auroraproduction.com

quiet moments
FOR SUCCESS
THE BAKER'S DOZEN

SELECTIONS BY ABI MAY

ACKNOWLEDGEMENTS

Quiet Moments collections have been derived largely from *Activated*, an international magazine published since 1995, edited by Keith Phillips. Alex Peterson is an *Activated* staff writer, and Abi May is a frequent contributor.

Quotations attributed to Jesus but not followed by Bible references are excerpts of personal messages that individuals received from Jesus while in prayer.

Aurora Production AG would like to thank all those who submitted their writings and prayers for publication; copyright holders have been identified where possible and we apologize for any inadvertent omissions.

CONTENTS

Foreword

Success takes many forms, and the ways and means to succeed are likewise varied. Yet although details differ, there are principles that can apply along the road to almost any achievement. This book offers thirteen principles to consider.

Thirteen is the number of the "baker's dozen": It was the practice of bakers in medieval Britain to give an extra loaf of bread when selling a dozen loaves, to avoid accusations of selling short weight. There is no short weight in these pages, but thirteen facets of success explored through a range of original thoughts, anecdotes, quotations, scriptures, and inspirational messages.

Each chapter stands alone so there is no need to go through this book in any order. Read a few pages at a time, or an entire chapter. Apply these principles to your dreams and goals, and let your quiet moments contribute to your own success.

Abi May
October 2011

CHAPTER 1

Portraits of Success

EVERY GOOD TREE BEARS GOOD FRUIT.
Matthew 7:17

There is a common force that drives most of us: we want to be successful. Regardless of who we are or what our specific goals may be, we want the security and comfort that material success provides, as well as the satisfaction of knowing that our lives are turning out well and count for something.

If we all want the same basic thing, why then are some people so much more successful than others? Circumstances alone aren't the deciding factor, because some people succeed despite incredibly difficult circumstances. Neither is success determined by natural ability alone, because many gifted people fail, while others who seem less likely to succeed do.

What, then, makes the difference? Some experts say it comes down to organization—establishing priorities, planning, managing time wisely, and so on. Others say creativity is the key, or motivation, or hard work, or single-mindedness, or the ability to work well with others. In reality, to have the greatest chance at success, it takes a combination of these and more. Success, it turns out, is a tricky matter.

Who can help you put it all together?—Who better than God? Look at the balance of His creation. From the tiny atom to the far reaches of the universe, can you imagine anything more intricate, efficient, or enduring? And who has more or better ideas than Him? Or who knows you and your needs better than Him?

And here's the best part: He wants to help you succeed. He says, "I know the thoughts that I think toward you, thoughts of peace and not of evil, to give you a future and a hope,"[1] so "commit to the Lord whatever you do, and your plans will succeed."[2] You and God can make an unstoppable combination.

Keith Phillips ■

[1] Jeremiah 29:11

[2] Proverbs 16:3 (NIV 1984)

Perspective adjustment

During an especially busy time, I had a perspective adjustment that changed my outlook for the better.

I was involved in several major projects, had a huge amount of work to do, and was quite tired—almost exhausted.

The verse that came to mind and changed my attitude about my circumstances was, "I beseech you therefore, brethren, by the mercies of God, that you present your bodies a living sacrifice, holy, acceptable to God, which is your reasonable service."[1] I realized that the long hours of work, the tiredness, and the difficult decisions I faced were all part of my "reasonable service."

Most of us have responsibilities that are sometimes difficult and trying. We all face situations that are challenging or cost us personally. We all have times when we feel so tired we think we can't go on.

Some of the great men and women of God, our forefathers in the faith—people like Abraham, Moses, Peter, and Paul, as well as outstanding Christians down through the ages such as David

Livingstone and Mother Teresa—made great sacrifices and endured many hardships and sorrows during their lifetimes. They repeatedly suffered poor health, many of them experienced loneliness, some of them struggled with depression, and they sometimes worked years on end without seeing much in the way of results. When we look at our situations from that perspective, it helps to see some of the things we go through in a different light.

The verse that comes right after "present your bodies a living sacrifice" says, "Be transformed by the renewing of your mind."[2] That verse applies well to having the right perspective on the sacrifices we make. If we have a realistic and yet also positive, praiseful attitude, it can make a big difference. When our perspective is renewed and realigned with the Lord's, it does literally transform our life.

So whenever you are tempted to feel that life is too rough, try to look at the sacrifices you have to make through this new perspective. When you do, you can't help but see things more positively.

Peter Amsterdam ■

[1] Romans 12:1

[2] Romans 12:2

As it will be

SEE HOW THE FARMER WAITS FOR THE PRECIOUS FRUIT OF THE
EARTH, WAITING PATIENTLY FOR IT UNTIL IT RECEIVES
THE EARLY AND LATTER RAIN.

James 5:7

I listened to a song demo today. I'd heard plenty of them before, but this one sounded unusually rough. I tried not to let on that it grated on my nerves. My friend had warned me that it was a demo before he pressed the play button, but I still wasn't quite prepared. I hoped he hadn't noticed me cringe or squirm in my chair.

After about a minute of private anguish, Jesus managed to get through to me.

It's just a demo, He spoke to my mind.

I know, I replied, *but it's still difficult to listen to.*

You have to hear it as the composer hears it—as it will be, not as it is now.

That's an interesting way to look at it.

Yes, and also the best way. It's how I look at you, actually.

Ouch! *Alright, I'll give it a try.*

To my astonishment, it worked instantly. When I listened beyond the rough background noises, the missed beats, and the off-key notes, the song was actually quite good. The melody, it turned out, was beautiful and relaxing, and it fit the lyrics perfectly. I looked forward to the finished product, and I told my friend so.

Throughout life, people make mistakes; they say or do some things wrong, and sometimes repeatedly or with disastrous results. That's because we are all rough demos in God's hands right now. There's a lot about each of us that He still needs to fix, and it's going to take time.

When we can look at others that way, when we try to see them not as they are, but as they will be, everyone wins. They have leeway to be less than perfect, learn by trial and error, and thus keep growing; and we can better appreciate the God-given beauty in those around us.

Peter Story ∎

Whatever a man sows, that he will also reap.
Galatians 6:7

Never let go of hope. One day you will see that it all has
finally come together. What you have always wished for has
finally come to be. You will look back and laugh
at what has passed and you will ask yourself,
How did I get through all of that?
Author unknown

The credo of some seems to be "All is fair in love, war,
business, and life," but what works is not always what's right.
Victories won immorally are shallow, usually short-lived, and
often have consequences that cancel any success.
Keith Phillips ■

Pearls

Success

Blessed be the LORD, who has given rest … according to all
that He promised. There has not failed one word
of all His good promise.

1 Kings 8:56

Then you will have good success.

Joshua 1:8

I will give you rain in its season, the land shall yield its
produce, and the trees of the field shall yield their fruit.

Leviticus 26:4

I will make you exceedingly fruitful.

Genesis 17:6

…He did good, gave us rain from heaven and fruitful seasons,
filling our hearts with food and gladness.

Acts 14:17

Live in me. Make your home in me just as I do in you. In the
same way that a branch can't bear grapes by itself but only by
being joined to the vine, you can't bear fruit unless you are
joined with me. … But if you make yourselves at home with
me and my words are at home in you, you can be sure that
whatever you ask will be listened to and acted upon.

John 15:4,7 (THE MESSAGE)

One's philosophy is not best
expressed in words; it is
expressed in the choices one
makes. In the long run, we
shape our lives and we shape
ourselves. The process never
ends until we die. And the
choices we make are ultimately
our own responsibility.
Eleanor Roosevelt

Do not throw away your
confidence; it will be
richly rewarded. You need
to persevere so that when
you have done the will of
God, you will receive what
he has promised.

Hebrews 10:35–36 (NIV)

CHAPTER 2

Possibilities Are Limitless

NOW FAITH IS THE SUBSTANCE OF THINGS HOPED FOR, THE
EVIDENCE OF THINGS NOT SEEN.
Hebrews 11:1

Learn from yesterday, live for today, hope for tomorrow.
Attributed to Albert Einstein

An optimist sees an opportunity in every calamity;
a pessimist sees a calamity in every opportunity.
Sir Winston Churchill

If an idea is like a spark, enthusiasm is the wind
that whips it into a bonfire strong enough
to withstand the rain of adversity.
Keith Phillips

When "reality" is not reality

WITH MEN IT IS IMPOSSIBLE, BUT NOT WITH GOD;
FOR WITH GOD ALL THINGS ARE POSSIBLE.
Mark 10:27

Sometimes, because you see yourself or situations a certain way, you put limits on what I am able to do in answer to your prayers. Sometimes your desire to want to be realistic and not get your hopes too high becomes a lack of faith. It's good to not have unrealistic expectations of yourself or life in general, but too much realism can lead to a defeatist attitude.

Being so "realistic" can dry up the soul. Put your hope and faith in Me. That's the only way you can be sure to not be disappointed.

There are times when the reality you see is not reality. But whether the challenge is in your mind or a real obstacle or circumstance, I can see you through it. I'm even able to defy the laws of nature in answer to your prayers, because all things are possible for Me. That's reality!

A message from Jesus received in prayer ■

Defy the impossible

JESUS SAID TO HIM, "IF YOU CAN BELIEVE, ALL THINGS
ARE POSSIBLE TO HIM WHO BELIEVES."
Mark 9:23

Have you ever read something and had it get stuck in your head?
That happened to me recently with a magazine article titled "Murder
of the Impossible." As soon as my eyes fell on it, I was intrigued.
(The word "murder" does have a way of capturing your attention!) I
quickly skimmed the text. It told of a man who had climbed most
of the highest mountains in the world. In fact, he had dedicated
his entire life to his dream of becoming one of the most skilled
and accomplished mountain climbers ever. His passion was not
without its price, though. Taking on the elements often cost him
his health, and on one such occasion frostbite claimed seven of his
toes. Undeterred, he continued to search for new ways to defy the
impossible.

After I put the magazine down, I reflected on what it means to defy the impossible. First of all, what is impossible? From the most innocent child to the wisest elder, we all encounter things that at first seem impossible to us. But unlike those who have been persuaded by experience that it doesn't pay to try to tackle the "impossible," babies expect to overcome. That's because they have a quality that the doubters lost as they grew up—childlike faith and trust. They have faith in their parents and trust them to be there to catch them if they fall. And their faith pays off; they learn to overcome an amazing assortment of obstacles, one step at a time.

That, I was reminded in my moment of reflection, is the key to vanquishing the impossible—faith in God. As we take God's hand, He can help us overcome any impossibility. Throughout history great men and women have confronted the impossible and have come out victorious, and that is why they are still remembered. The road to victory was long and treacherous, but they went the distance, one step at a time. They defeated the impossible because they held on, and when that victory was theirs they looked ahead to the next challenge and moved on.

When the impossibilities of life loom large, take God's hand and take it one step at a time. He makes the impossible possible.

Ariana Andreassen ■

The China Doll

YOU CROWN THE YEAR WITH YOUR GOODNESS,
AND YOUR PATHS DRIP WITH ABUNDANCE.

Psalm 65:11

When my older brother was 13, he had an unusual hobby. We called it dumpster diving. A nearby apartment complex housed college students from around the country, and at the end of the school year the students would discard everything they didn't want to haul home with them, including quite a few items that still had some value. My brother capitalized on the opportunity.

One day, he brought home a China Doll plant, which he gave to me. My mom, who has a green thumb, said it was a good find. I moved it to my room, and would set it out on the front porch every few days for some sunshine. After I'd had the plant for a few months, its leaves started drooping and then falling off. Within a couple of weeks, there were no leaves left. When I asked my mom what was wrong, she said it might have gone into hibernation. A plant without leaves held no interest for me, so I put it in the back yard with my mom's other potted plants. It stayed there for quite some time, leafless and forlorn.

One day my mom brought a plant to my room. Yes, it was my China Doll, and there were tiny sprouts at the tips of its branches. Over the next weeks, the sprouts grew into new shoots and leaves, and eventually my plant was in full bloom again. This cycle continued over the years.

I eventually moved away from home and left the China Doll with my mom and her green thumb. In one letter my mom wrote: "I thought your China Doll had finally died. I almost tossed it, but you know how I hate to throw away a plant. I waited a while and sure enough, it grew back fuller than ever."

The following spring I went to visit my mom. She had more time for gardening now that most of her kids had moved away, and the back yard was beautiful, full of aromatic rose bushes and flower-covered arbors and trellises. There on the porch, transplanted into a bigger pot, sat my China Doll. It was at least four feet tall.

They say that one man's trash is another man's treasure. That China Doll will always hold a special place in my heart, not because I'm sentimental about a plant, but because it taught me to hope.

Some things seem to be hibernating—a few dreams and goals—but with the sunshine of God's love, the water of His Word, and a little of His tender loving care, they will blossom in His good time.

Bonita Hele ■

MY GOD SHALL SUPPLY ALL YOUR NEED ACCORDING TO HIS
RICHES IN GLORY BY CHRIST JESUS.
Philippians 4:19

God is in the heavenly realm, but He works in the real world. He deals not just in spiritual blessings and rewards, but in tangible, black-and-white, dollars-and-cents material blessings and rewards as well. He's the God of heaven, and also the God of this present world. He transcends both, rules in both, lives in both, dominates both, creates in both, and has the power to pay us in both currencies.

We need to learn to trust Him for the material things that we need—not just our spiritual needs like happiness, purpose, and peace of mind. He's just as powerful, just as capable, and just as willing to give us the tangible, practical blessings we need. We need to not limit God in our minds, but realize that His influence is all encompassing and that He is capable of performing miracles in both the spiritual and physical realms. He can and will give us both spiritual and material blessings, and we all need a whole lot of both.

Peter Amsterdam ■

[JESUS] SAID TO HIM, "FOLLOW ME." SO HE AROSE
AND FOLLOWED HIM.
Matthew 9:9

What's the difference between religion and Jesus? Perhaps you've heard this analogy: "Religion is us reaching up to God; Jesus is God reaching down to us." That's true, but there is a lot more to the second part than most people realize. We make contact with God through His Son, Jesus, when we receive Him as our Savior, but while salvation is a one-time thing, our contact with Jesus isn't meant to be. Neither is it meant to be a once-a-week or once-in-a-blue-moon thing. It's meant to be a daily thing—direct, personal, daily contact that develops over time into a deep, vibrant, and mutually satisfying relationship.

By the time most of us discover that Jesus is alive and cares about us personally, though, we've spent years trying to make our way through life on our own. Because we've become more or less self-sufficient and comfortable with reality as we've always perceived it, in a world without Jesus, it often comes as a whole new thought that we can involve Him in our everyday decisions and activities. This brings us to what is possibly the second most important decision we will ever make, after receiving Jesus: Will we welcome Him into our everyday life so our relationship can grow and He can bless us to the full? Or will we continue to live in our shadow reality, relying on our own reasoning, experience, and other resources? That's a decision we all make every day, consciously or unconsciously.

It takes effort to change our habits and thought patterns to include Jesus more, but the rewards are out of this world. Every time we reach out to Him by turning our thoughts into conversations with Jesus, He's there to listen and help us in wonderful and often surprising ways. Make a little more room for Jesus every day, and every day will be better than the day before!

Keith Phillips ∎

No limits

I can't remember ever seeing a flea circus—the classic sideshow event in which fleas are the performers—but I came across a fascinating article about how the fleas are trained.

Fleas can jump extraordinarily high, relative to their tiny size. Training fleas involves putting them into a small box or jar. Without a lid, the fleas could easily jump out, so the flea trainer puts a lid in place and waits.

Inside the container, the fleas jump up in order to escape. They hit the lid and fall back down. Again and again, the fleas will jump, hit the lid, and fall back. Then, after some time, the fleas don't jump so high. They jump up almost as high as the lid, but not quite.

Eventually, the trainer will remove the lid. The fleas could easily escape now, but they don't even try. They've become accustomed to only jumping to a certain height. They have more or less decided that's their limit; they are going as high as they can go, and they don't attempt anything further. Freedom is just a jump away, but it's a jump they don't make. "Stupid fleas," we say. "So void of intelligence that they don't realize the lid has been removed."

But come to think of it, we too sometimes allow ourselves to be limited by barriers that exist only in our minds. We tried and failed at something, and our confidence was shaken. The next time around, when an opportunity arose to try something new or bigger, we didn't rise to the challenge because we didn't think we were capable of doing it.

Life is full of new beginnings and fresh possibilities. The lesson of the fleas should not be lost on us. We don't have to let the setbacks or mistakes of the past hold us down, like the nonexistent lid on the fleas' jar. No imaginary limits for us! With God's help, we can rise to new heights.

Abi May ■

CHAPTER 3

Partnerships: Teamwork

NO ONE CAN WHISTLE A SYMPHONY.
IT TAKES AN ORCHESTRA TO PLAY IT.
Halfrod Luccock

Two are better than one,
Because they have a good reward for their labor.
For if they fall, one will lift up his companion.
But woe to him who is alone when he falls,
For he has no one to help him up.
Again, if two lie down together, they will keep warm;
But how can one be warm alone?
Though one may be overpowered by another,
two can withstand him.
And a threefold cord is not quickly broken.
Ecclesiastes 4:9–12

By this we know love, because He laid down His life for us.
And we also ought to lay down our lives
for the brethren.
1 John 3:16

Lord, help me live from day to day
In such a self-forgetful way
That even when I kneel to pray
My prayer shall be for others.

Help me in all the work I do
To ever be sincere and true
And know that all I'd do for You
Must needs be done for others.

Let self be crucified and slain
And buried deep, and all in vain
May efforts be to rise again,
Unless to live for others.

And when my work on earth is done,
And my new work in Heav'n's begun,
May I forget the crown I've won,
While thinking still of others.

Others, Lord, yes others,
Let this my motto be,
Help me to live for others,
That I may live like Thee.
Charles D. Meigs ■

THIS IS THE MESSAGE THAT YOU HEARD FROM THE BEGINNING,
THAT WE SHOULD LOVE ONE ANOTHER.

1 John 3:11

A team of songwriters, musicians, and singers had worked well together on various projects over the space of several years. They were a rather motley crew and had had their share of ups and downs, but had always managed to hang together somehow. So when nearly everyone's inspiration level hit an unprecedented and inexplicable low at the same time, the couple leading the team was naturally concerned. They were Christians who depended a lot on prayer, so they asked God to show them what had gone wrong and how to turn things around.

The answer they received was short and simple: "You've been cutting corners on love." Everyone had gotten so wrapped up in their work that they'd all stopped taking time to show one another love and appreciation—the very things that had made them such a good team in the first place.

The couple explained that to the rest of the team, and together they drew up a list of all the special little things they'd stopped saying or doing for each other. Then at the end of the meeting they all prayed that Jesus would help them take more time to show love. It wasn't long before the team produced its best music ever. They had found the secret to staying close as a team and keeping the inspiration level high. It was in little daily deeds of kindness and caring.

We're not all songwriters, musicians, or singers, of course, but there is hardly a person on earth who isn't part of at least one team—a family, a marriage, a business partnership, a staff, a work crew, a sports team, a club, or a circle of friends. "No man is an island." We all need others, and we all have an opportunity to better the people and situations around us. Love and communication are the keys, and, as always, God wants nothing less than the best for all of us. As you help Him bring out the best in others, He'll bring out the best in you.

Keith Phillips ■

Some people
dream of success,
while others
wake up and
work hard at it.
Author unknown

Walk boldly
and wisely.
There is a hand
above that will
help you on.
Philip James Bailey

Bring out the best

One quality that good leaders seem to have in common is the ability to bring out the best in others. Whether they are bosses, managers, team captains, or role models, inevitably they have learned to not think in terms of problems, but rather in terms of people and their potential.

When those leaders see others doing something wrong or working inefficiently, rather than fuming or stepping in to do the job themselves, they challenge those people to keep trying until they get it right, and then praise them when they do.

The bosses could probably do those particular tasks better or quicker, but if they made a habit of that, they would end up trying to do everything themselves. When there is a lot to do, the leader needs to delegate, and that involves trust, belief, training, and commendation. The leader needs to provide whatever training may be missing and trust the work to others; the people doing the work need to believe they can succeed; and then the leader needs to commend the effort, even if it's not perfect. Over time, the people doing the work will usually learn to get it right, but not many will continue to try their best if all they hear is what they did wrong or how they could have done better.

No matter how otherwise talented leaders may be, if they can't work well with people they will soon find themselves disliked and distrusted by those they are trying to lead. People trust those who they know care about them, and such trust is built by their leader taking a personal interest, showing concern, and being generous with praise and appreciation. People who consistently get those types of positive reinforcement usually do their best to live up to their boss's expectations.

The people expert Dale Carnegie gave an example of a boss who understood that principle. Gunter Schmidt was a store manager, and he had a problem: one of his employees was careless about putting the correct prices on the display shelves. Reminders and admonitions didn't work, so after receiving one too many customer complaints Schmidt finally called the employee into his office. Rather than giving her the telling-off she expected, however, he told her that he was appointing her "supervisor of price tag posting" for the entire store. It was now her responsibility to keep all the shelves properly tagged—and she fulfilled that role satisfactorily from that day on. All she had needed was for her boss to express trust by giving her a little more responsibility.

Tina Kapp ■

The love catalyst

REGARDING LIFE TOGETHER AND GETTING ALONG WITH EACH
OTHER, YOU DON'T NEED ME TO TELL YOU WHAT TO DO. YOU'RE
GOD-TAUGHT IN THESE MATTERS. JUST LOVE ONE ANOTHER!
1 Thessalonians 4:9 (THE MESSAGE)

Everyone has good qualities. Find specific things about others that you can sincerely compliment them on, and be generous with your praise. If you can't find anything right off, look deeper. Ask God to show you the positive qualities that must be there, because He sees things worth loving and praising in everyone. The harder it is to find that special something, the greater the reward is likely to be for both you and the other person when you do. If you can find even a threadlike vein and shine a little love on it in the form of praise, it can lead you straight to the mother lode. People will open up to you, and you'll discover lots of wonderful things about them.

Shannon Shayler ∎

Working well

LET YOUR SPEECH ALWAYS BE WITH GRACE, SEASONED WITH
SALT, THAT YOU MAY KNOW HOW YOU OUGHT
TO ANSWER EACH ONE.
Colossians 4:6

Misunderstandings are unpleasant under any circumstances,
but especially so in the workplace, which is often already stressful.
Building good working relationships takes time, so be patient. Here
are a few tips that should help.

1. One thing at a time. Give the business at hand and those you
are talking with your undivided attention.

2. Listen. Hear your colleagues out before expressing your own
thoughts and opinions, and never interrupt. This will not only help
you benefit from their experience, but it is a way of showing respect,
which wins respect.

3. Ask for more information or a clarification, if necessary. A
lot of communication problems stem from people being too proud to
say they need more background information or don't understand the
point someone else is trying to make.

4. Think things through. Know what you want to get across before you start to speak. This will help you be clearer, more specific, and more direct in your presentation, and therefore less likely to be misunderstood.

5. Don't over-communicate. As John Kotter put it, "Good communication does not mean that you have to speak in perfectly formed sentences and paragraphs. It isn't about slickness. Simple and clear go a long way."

6. Acknowledge your limitations. Don't be afraid to say "I don't know."

7. Watch your unspoken communications. Nearly everything you do communicates something to others. Punctuality communicates. Attentiveness communicates. Body language communicates. Your facial expression communicates. Your tone of voice communicates. Even silence communicates. Positive signals open lines of communication; negative signals hinder.

8. Be sympathetic. To understand others, try to put yourself in their position. Why do they think or act the way they do? Be careful not to misread others' body language. If you're not sure, ask.

9. Strive for unity. It's easier to work with people than it is to work when at odds with them. Avoid conflicts and personality clashes by looking for common ground and admirable qualities in those you work with.

10. Be positive. Build team spirit by dwelling on jobs well done and progress being made toward your united goals. Focus on problems from the angle of "how can we fix this" rather than "who's to blame."

Alex Peterson ■

Better as a team

God composed the body, having given greater honor to that
part which lacks it, that there should be no schism in the
body, but that the members should have the same care for one
another. And if one member suffers, all the members
suffer with it; or if one member is honored,
all the members rejoice with it.
1 Corinthians 12:24–26

Teamwork is the fuel that allows common people
to attain uncommon results.
Andrew Carnegie

No member of a crew is praised for the rugged
individuality of his rowing.
Ralph Waldo Emerson

If I could solve all the problems myself, I would.
*Thomas Edison, when asked why he had a team
of twenty-one assistants* ■

Appreciation in the workplace

Appreciation is a human need. It's not just something that's nice to have when possible, but something that each person needs in order to be happy and to thrive. That's true in every setting, but it's perhaps nowhere more evident than in the workplace. When people feel genuinely appreciated by those they work for and with, they're much more likely to be excellent contributors and "team players."

When there's lots of appreciation flowing between team members, this significantly boosts the chances of that team becoming a winning team. Appreciation has the power to bring out the best in people. It makes them want to do more, stretch more, contribute more, feel like they're capable of more, and be content in the role they play. If everyone on the team appreciates one another, respects one another, and shows faith in one another, this multiplies the overall productivity and happiness of the team.

Thinking positive thoughts about one another is good, it's a start, but if we don't express those thoughts, if we don't take the time or make the effort to verbalize them, they won't do anyone else any good. We can't expect people to read our minds. We have to put those thoughts into words or actions. We have to be active in our appreciation.

There's so much that we can appreciate others for, but it takes effort on our part. We have to get closer to people and talk to them more and on a deeper level. We need to try to expand our "appreciation horizons" and not only appreciate others for the things that benefit us in the most obvious, direct ways. It means so much to people when someone takes an interest in them, notices unique and special things about them, and takes appreciation to a deeper level.

No matter what may have held you back from dishing out sincere and regular appreciation in the past, you can begin today to bring out the best in others by pointing it out. Appreciate always.

Maria Fontaine ■

CHAPTER 4

Power: Getting God's help

JESUS LOOKED AT THEM AND SAID, "WITH MEN IT IS
IMPOSSIBLE, BUT NOT WITH GOD; FOR WITH GOD
ALL THINGS ARE POSSIBLE."

Mark 10:27

For all the negative things we say to ourselves, God has given us His positive responses in the Bible.

You say, "It's impossible."
God says, "All things are possible with Me."—*Matthew 19:26*

You say, "I'm so tired."
God says, "I will give you rest."—*Matthew 11:28–30*

You say, "Nobody really loves me."
God says, "I love you."—*John 3:16 and 13:34*

You say, "I can't go on."
God says, "My grace is sufficient and I will always be there to help you."—*2 Corinthians 12:9 and Psalm 91:15*

You say, "I can't figure things out."
God says, "I will direct your steps."—*Proverbs 3:5–6*

You say, "I can't do this."
God says, "You don't have to do it.—I will."—*2 Chronicles 20:17*

You say, "It's not worth it."
God says, "It will be worth it."—*Romans 8:18*

You say, "I can't forgive myself."
God says, "I forgive you."—*1 John 1:9 and Romans 8:1*

You say, "I can't manage."
God says, "I will supply all your needs."—*Philippians 4:19*

You say, "I'm not able."
God says, "You can do it with My help."—*Philippians 4:13 and 2 Corinthians 3:5*

You say, "I'm afraid."
God says, "Be not afraid, for I am with you."—*Jeremiah 42:11*

You say, "I'm always worried and frustrated."
God says, "Give your cares to Me."—*1 Peter 5:7*

You say, "I don't have enough faith."
God says, "I've given everyone a measure of faith."—*Romans 12:3*

You say, "I'm not smart enough."
God says, "I give you wisdom."—*James 1:5 and 1 Corinthians 1:30*

You say, "I feel all alone."
God says, "I will never leave you or forsake you."—*Hebrews 13:5*

Author unknown ■

Itaipu Dam, on a stretch of the Paraná River that forms the boundary between Brazil and Paraguay, is the world's largest operational hydroelectric power plant. In 1995, a decade after it opened, the U.S. magazine Popular Mechanics listed it as one of the seven wonders of the modern world. By 2000 it was generating over 90 billion kilowatt-hours of power each year, enough to supply 93% of the electrical power consumed by Paraguay's 5.5 million people and 20% of that consumed by Brazil's 184 million. That's a lot of power! The river flowed there for thousands of years before the dam, of course, which means that the potential for all that power was also there, untapped, until someone set out to harness it.

The spiritual power that God makes available to us can be likened to that river: There is tremendous potential there, but it doesn't do us any good until we acknowledge its existence, recognize its potential, and learn to use it. If we've gone all of our lives without that spiritual power, and if we've managed okay and been relatively happy, maybe things will work out fine if we continue as we have. Maybe that wouldn't be so bad. But we would never know what we would be missing, and we would be missing a lot!

Itaipu Dam wasn't the first of its kind, of course. Those who conceived and built it benefited from the knowledge and experience of many others, going all the way back to the first paddle wheel. Again, God's power is a bit like that. Men and women before us have learned how to draw on God's power, and we can benefit from and build on their knowledge and experience.

Keith Phillips ■

Work with Me

When you work with Me as your partner on the job, you're
working with the most multitalented, multitasking partner in the
universe. I truly can do anything and everything!

Look at Me not only as a spiritual guide and counselor, but as
someone who can actually get in there, roll up His sleeves, and help
you do the work. I can save you hours and hours of work time by
taking care of the behind-the-scenes side of things. I will even take
care of situations before you have to get involved.

Tell Me specifically what you want to see done, and leave it with
Me. Don't worry or fret about it, and don't keep checking up on Me
to see if I'm on the job. Of course I'm on the job! Have faith, and
your faith will bring out an entirely new dynamic in our relationship.

This is the key to your success: Let Me carry a good chunk of the
load, which is exactly what I want to do. Commit things to Me in
prayer. Depend on Me, and let Me do the "heavy lifting." I can easily
remove obstacles that look insurmountable to you and help things to
fall into place as they should. Give Me a chance to help you out, to
do some of the work.

A message from Jesus received in prayer ■

I am willing to
go anywhere,
anywhere,
anywhere—so long
as it's forward.
David Livingstone

The road to success is not
to be run upon by seven-
leagued boots. Step by step,
little by little, bit by bit—that
is the way to wealth, that is
the way to wisdom, that is
the way to glory.
Charles Buxton

Getting God's input

SPEAK, LORD, FOR YOUR SERVANT HEARS.
1 Samuel 3:9

Is God personally concerned about you? Does He want to provide solutions to your problems, bless your endeavors, help you get the most out of life, and make you the best person you can possibly be? If so, is He able to tell you how? Yes, yes, and yes!

He knows that you have questions and problems, and He wants to give you answers and solutions. To that end, He created a means of two-way communication, a channel between Him and you, so that you can talk to Him in prayer and in return receive messages that He speaks directly to and specially for you.

Even if you don't consider yourself very spiritual or close to God, you'll be happy to know that God will speak to anyone who has even only a little childlike faith—and He wants to speak to you, to lead you into a closer relationship with Him and to improve your life in the process.

Start by finding a quiet place and taking a few minutes to talk to God, just like you would talk to a close friend. If you have a specific question, go ahead and ask. Or perhaps you don't have anything in particular on your mind, but want to hear whatever He might have to say to you. Either way, once you've told Him that you want to hear from Him, do your best to concentrate and listen with your spirit for His answer.

Sometimes God may speak by bringing to mind a familiar verse or passage from the Bible, which when applied to the particular situation you're asking Him about, can be the clear and simple answer that you need.

At other times, God may speak a new message—words that He's never spoken exactly that way to anyone else. The wording style may range from formal to casual, everyday language. God can express Himself any way He likes on any subject, but He usually speaks to us each in a way that will be easy for us to receive and relate to.

It's easy to dismiss this little inner voice as being your own thoughts, especially when you are first starting to hear from God, but it's important that you accept that this is Him speaking to you. When you've sincerely asked God to speak, He will. "Ask and it will be given to you."[1] He fills the spiritually hungry with good things.[2]

Try not to analyze, scrutinize, or judge the message as it is coming, as that will interrupt the flow. You should study it later, though, so unless His message is very short you will probably want to type or write it down as it comes, before you forget any of the details.

You may feel any one of a number of emotions while receiving a message from God. Some people feel a surge of excitement or joy, some feel nervous, some break down and cry—but many, perhaps even most, feel nothing unusual at all. Some may feel something sometimes and nothing at other times. Whether you feel something or not doesn't make the message you receive more or less valid. "We walk by faith, and not by sight"[3]—and certainly not by feelings!

Don't be disappointed if at first you don't receive long, eloquent messages from God, although that can happen. Usually with time and experience, as you exercise your gift of hearing from God, the messages you receive will become more detailed and more complete. Don't give up! Practice makes perfect.

Remember also that a message from heaven doesn't have to be lengthy to be exactly what He wants to tell you at that moment. Sometimes God may give you the answer you need in one sentence or less. Of course, it's good to wait long enough to make sure He doesn't have any more to say before going about your business, but once you feel that He has finished talking, then thank Him for speaking and trust that the message He gave you contains the answer you were asking Him for.

There will probably be times when you ask Him to speak but are too distracted by other thoughts to hear anything at all. Don't worry. It's tough to concentrate sometimes, and God understands our human weaknesses. If this is new to you, the simple fact that you're trying is a sign of progress. Keep it up!

Try to take a few minutes each day to pray and thank God for His goodness. Follow this with your "question of the day" and a few moments of listening for His answer or whatever else He may want to say to you. As you get in the habit of hearing from God, it will become easier. As you continue to strengthen your faith by reading God's written Word, and if you continue to earnestly desire this gift of His Spirit, God won't fail you. He has promised to speak to you, and He will!

Rafael Holding ■

[1] Matthew 7:7

[2] Luke 1:53

[3] 2 Corinthians 5:7

Hear from heaven
A SPIRITUAL EXERCISE

The Bible's book of 1 Kings includes the story of the prophet Elijah. Chapter 19 recounts the tumultuous episode when he was running for his life from wicked Queen Jezebel and hiding in the wilderness. After a while God led Elijah to go to Mount Horeb. There God told Elijah to leave the cave where he had taken refuge and stand before Him. A strong wind tore into the mountain and broke nearby rocks in pieces; then there was an earthquake; then a fire; then a "still small voice."[1] God was not in the wind, the earthquake, or the fire, but that still small voice was His.

You too can get alone with God to hear His voice and thereby receive His words of love and encouragement, answers to your questions, and solutions to your problems. Here's how:

Find a quiet place where you won't be disturbed, preferably for at least 15 minutes. Bring your Bible or some other inspirational reading, and a laptop or a pen and something to write on.

Begin by reading a short passage or two to boost your faith. Then think about a matter that you would like God to speak to you about—a problem or concern or even something that you're curious about. Sit quietly and listen to what He tells you. Perhaps He'll remind you of something you have read in His Word. Perhaps He'll remind you of something you have seen or something someone has said. Or perhaps He'll give you a message in words or pictures. Whatever comes to your mind, write it down for future reference, and then thank Him for speaking.

When you are first learning to tune in to His voice you may mistake it for your own thoughts, but with practice you will learn to distinguish between the two—especially when He tells you things you never would have thought of yourself.

Abi May ■

¹ 1 Kings 19:3–12

Quiet Moments for Success

GRACE AND PEACE BE MULTIPLIED TO YOU IN THE KNOWLEDGE
OF GOD AND OF JESUS OUR LORD, AS HIS DIVINE POWER
HAS GIVEN TO US ALL THINGS THAT PERTAIN TO LIFE AND
GODLINESS, THROUGH THE KNOWLEDGE OF HIM WHO CALLED
US BY GLORY AND VIRTUE, BY WHICH HAVE BEEN GIVEN TO US
EXCEEDINGLY GREAT AND PRECIOUS PROMISES, THAT THROUGH
THESE YOU MAY BE PARTAKERS OF THE DIVINE NATURE.

2 Peter 1:2–4

God has given us some amazing promises in His Word. These promises are for real. They have been given to us by our truthful God who never lies. He doesn't exaggerate. He doesn't pump up His promises to lift Himself up or to make us feel good. He gives us His promises because He wants us to believe and claim them as our own, so He can give us all of the great things He has in store for us.

They're not fake promises, but each one is conditional. "Delight yourself also in the Lord, and He shall give you the desires of your heart."[1] "Seek first the kingdom of God and His righteousness, and all these things shall be added to you."[2] "Give and it will be given to you."[3] "No good thing will He withhold from those who walk uprightly."[4]

They're each dependent on us fulfilling our part of the bargain, which nearly always comes down to keeping His two great commandments: Love God, and love our neighbors as we do ourselves.[5] But if we do our part, they are guaranteed to come to pass—not necessarily in the way we want or think they will, but in God's time and way. Like a wise and loving parent, He always knows what's best for us and is happy to give it to us. That's the God factor.

Peter Amsterdam ∎

[1] Psalm 37:4

[2] Matthew 6:33

[3] Luke 6:38

[4] Psalm 84:11

[5] Matthew 22:37–39

CHAPTER 5

Planning and Goals

HE WHO FAILS TO PLAN, PLANS TO FAIL.
Author unknown

For which of you, intending to build a tower, does not sit
down first and count the cost, whether he has enough to
finish it—lest, after he has laid the foundation, and is not
able to finish, all who see it begin to mock him, saying,
"This man began to build and was not able to finish"?
Luke 14:28–30

Where there is no vision, the people perish.
Proverbs 29:18 (KJV)

It's okay to dream of building castles in the air, but they won't become realities without a realistic step-by-step plan for putting them there. Today we have space stations, but they didn't just happen.
Keith Phillips

When making plans, we must remember that God is in control of the situation, and He is able to change people and situations and make things happen that are far beyond our abilities. That's the "God factor." What seems logical to the human mind often takes on a different perspective when the God factor comes into play. The God factor is that extra factor in the equation that overrides even the laws of nature and makes the impossible possible—and it is activated by our faith.
James Wyatt

Dust off those dreams, get God's promises and power behind you, and gear up for an exciting, successful future.
Keith Phillips ■

Climbing the year

THE LORD IS MY SHEPHERD; I SHALL NOT WANT.

Psalm 23:1

Even the best climbers need guides when they climb unfamiliar mountains. In fact, only a foolhardy novice would try to go without one—a novice like me.

Years ago I was on vacation in the Alps of Switzerland, and on the last day a friend and I decided to climb a nearby mountain. It was late afternoon by the time we got started, and we hadn't gone far before we passed a rugged shepherd on his way down with his sheep, after a day of grazing them further up the mountain. "Darkness comes early and suddenly in the mountains," he warned us. "Wait until tomorrow and hire a guide." But tomorrow would be too late. By the next afternoon we'd be on a train home, having missed a unique opportunity. Impetuously we trekked on.

As sure as night follows day, we were soon in near total darkness. Because it was overcast, there wasn't even any moonlight or starlight. We could barely make out the rocky trail right at our feet, let alone see the trail ahead. One misstep and we would go tumbling down the mountain. We would have to spend the night on the mountain.

We had one sleeping bag with us, so we decided to take turns sleeping in it.

Then it started to rain heavily. We were not only cold but also drenched, and so was our sleeping bag. We managed to take refuge under an outcropping of rock. After a long ordeal, dawn broke, the rain stopped, and we were able to make our descent.

On our way down the trail, we met the same shepherd we had talked to the previous afternoon. Seeing our sorry condition, he nodded and gave us a look that was a mix of amusement and relief. Had it gotten much colder that night, we could have died of exposure.

Taking on the challenges of the year is often likened to climbing a mountain: Although it's a lot of hard work and potentially dangerous, it holds special rewards for those who rise to the challenge and don't quit till they reach the summit.

But sometimes we may become too self-confident and feel that we can go it alone. If we're smart, we'll realize that we need the help of a mountain guide, and of course there's no better guide than Jesus, whom the Bible calls the "Chief Shepherd" of our souls.[1] He knows where the green pastures are, as well as where the dangers lie. If we stay close to Him, He will help us to reach our goals for the coming year, to conquer the summit and experience the thrill of victory.

Curtis Peter van Gorder ■

[1] 1 Peter 5:4

Staying in touch

I LOVE THOSE WHO LOVE ME,
AND THOSE WHO SEEK ME DILIGENTLY WILL FIND ME.
Proverbs 8:17

Talk to Me and I will talk to you. It's that simple. I'm here. I'm always with you. If you want to talk to Me, I'm available anytime and anywhere. I don't have office hours or office fees. I don't even have an office. I am available for you whenever you need Me. If you will stop, acknowledge Me, speak to Me, and wait, I will answer. I will never leave you comfortless.[1] I will never leave you without an answer. I will never walk away from you. I am here for you.

A message from Jesus received in prayer ■

---

[1] John 14:18 (KJV)

Choice and decision-making

For the best results, pray for God's guidance.

> In all your ways acknowledge Him,
> And He shall direct your paths.
> *Proverbs 3:6*

> Commit your works to the LORD,
> And your thoughts will be established.
> *Proverbs 16:3*

> Trust in the LORD with all your heart,
> And lean not on your own understanding.
> *Proverbs 3:5*

Our own thoughts and reasoning can lead us astray.

> There are many plans in a man's heart,
> Nevertheless the LORD's counsel—that will stand.
> *Proverbs 19:21*

"For My thoughts are not your thoughts,
Nor are your ways My ways," says the LORD.
"For as the heavens are higher than the earth,
So are My ways higher than your ways,
And My thoughts than your thoughts."
Isaiah 55:8–9

O LORD, I know the way of man is not in himself;
It is not in man who walks to direct his own steps.
Jeremiah 10:23

God helps us make the best choice.

Who is the man that fears the LORD?
Him shall He teach in the way He chooses.
Psalm 25:12

I will instruct you and teach you in the way you should go;
I will guide you with My eye.
Psalm 32:8

For I know the thoughts that I think toward you,
says the LORD, thoughts of peace and not of evil,
to give you a future and a hope.

Jeremiah 29:11

Sound decisions are based on God's Word.

Your word is a lamp to my feet
And a light to my path.

Psalm 119:105

Your testimonies also are my delight
And my counselors.

Psalm 119:24

Direct my steps by Your word.

Psalm 119:133

All Scripture is given by inspiration of God,
and is profitable for doctrine, for reproof, for correction,
for instruction in righteousness.

2 Timothy 3:16 ■

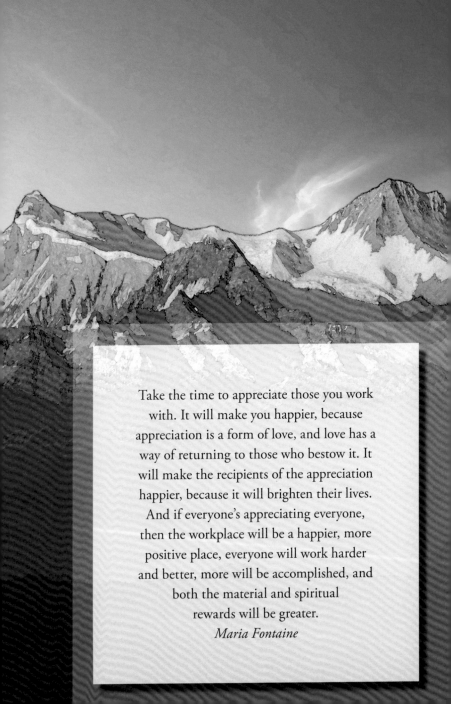

Take the time to appreciate those you work with. It will make you happier, because appreciation is a form of love, and love has a way of returning to those who bestow it. It will make the recipients of the appreciation happier, because it will brighten their lives. And if everyone's appreciating everyone, then the workplace will be a happier, more positive place, everyone will work harder and better, more will be accomplished, and both the material and spiritual rewards will be greater.

Maria Fontaine

Coming together
is a beginning.
Keeping together
is progress.
Working together
is success.
Henry Ford

Making great decisions

Perfect decisions are few and far between because life is messy. A great decision is always possible, however. Great decisions don't all have fairytale endings, but they do achieve the best possible outcome under the circumstances.

The most successful decision-makers don't act on impulse, intuition, or even experience alone; they have a system that they work through step by step. Here is one such system:

Define the issue. A problem well stated is a problem half solved. Employ the "who, what, when, why, and how" regimen of the journalist, although not necessarily in that order. Why is the decision necessary? What is the objective? How can a great decision change things for the better? Whom will it affect? When does it need to be made?

Take a positive approach. Make a conscious effort to see the situation as an opportunity rather than a problem.

List your options. The more alternatives you consider, the more likely you will be to not overlook the best solution.

Gather information about your options. You will not only make better decisions if you have investigated thoroughly, but you will also have more peace of mind as you carry out your decision.

Be objective. If you already have an opinion on the matter, the natural tendency will be to look primarily for evidence to confirm that opinion. That works if you happen to be right, but if you're not… Welcome alternatives and opposing views. Remind yourself that the goal is not to prove yourself right, but to make the right decision.

Consider your options. Write down the pros and cons for each option and see how they stack up against each other. Try to determine both best-case and worst-case scenarios for each option. See if there is some way to combine several promising solutions into one potent solution.

Be true to yourself. Do any of the alternatives compromise your values? If so, scratch them from the list.

Make a decision. When you're convinced that you've found the best alternative, commit to it.

Be open to change if circumstances change. Once you make a decision and begin to act on it, a better option may open up. This is sometimes referred to as the "boat-and-rudder effect." It's not until a boat is in motion that the rudder can come into play, but when it does, it makes greater maneuverability possible.

Ask Jesus. Last but certainly not least, pray for guidance at each step of the decision-making process. The answers to all your questions and problems are simple for Jesus, so if you're smart, you'll be like the man who said, "I may not know all the answers, but I know the Answer Man!" Jesus has all the answers. He is the answer!

Alex Peterson ∎

Pearls

Our needs

My God shall supply all your need according to
His riches in glory by Christ Jesus.
Philippians 4:19

Seek first the kingdom of God and His righteousness,
and all these things shall be added to you.
Matthew 6:33

The young lions lack and suffer hunger;
But those who seek the LORD shall not lack any good thing.
Psalm 34:10

For the LORD God is a sun and shield;
The LORD will give grace and glory;
No good thing will He withhold
From those who walk uprightly.
Psalm 84:11

Ask, and it will be given to you; seek, and you will find;
knock, and it will be opened to you. For everyone who asks
receives, and he who seeks finds, and to him
who knocks it will be opened.
Matthew 7:7–8 ∎

Meet Me in the morning

NOW IN THE MORNING, HAVING RISEN A LONG WHILE BEFORE
DAYLIGHT, HE WENT OUT AND DEPARTED TO A SOLITARY
PLACE; AND THERE HE PRAYED.
Mark 1:35

You do well to take time with Me first thing in the morning, for
you are powerless without the strength you draw from Me, you are
foolish without the wisdom you learn from Me, and you have no love
to share with others unless you first get it from Me. Without Me, you
would continue on in your own little world and be limited to your
own meager resources. Your human strength would run out before
the day had scarcely started, your own thoughts would get in the
way, and you wouldn't go far on yesterday's store of love. But when
you come to Me, I open the boundless world of My Spirit to you. I
am wisdom, I am strength, and I am love.

As I told My disciples, you can find rest for your spirit and
strength for the day in Me.[1] It seems easier to carry on in your own
energy than to work at entering into the realm of My Spirit where I
would carry you along, but that's not so. You really make it harder
for yourself, because you make it harder for Me to help you.

So take a little time each morning to draw close to Me. Practice
makes perfect. As you practice reaching out to Me by praying and
reading My Word, it will become easier. Keep taking this time with
Me each morning and it will become easier to connect with Me
throughout the day, whenever you need My help.

A message from Jesus received in prayer ■

[1] Matthew 11:28–30

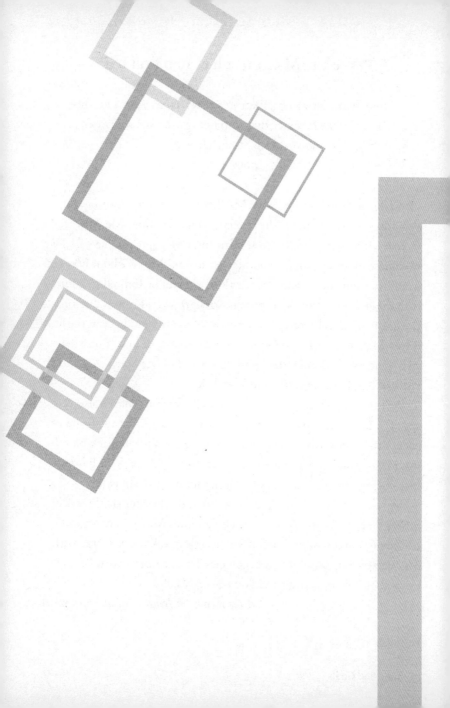

CHAPTER 6

Practical Steps to Success

COMMIT YOUR WAY TO THE LORD,
TRUST ALSO IN HIM,
AND HE SHALL BRING IT TO PASS.
Psalm 37:5

Strategies for success

Faced with a major project or challenge? You probably have a general idea of where you want to go, but you'll need a strategy, a plan of steps to take in order to reach that objective.

Planning is an investment. To plan wisely and well takes time, effort, patience, good research, and counsel—and for those of us who include a spiritual dimension, time in prayer. But a well-formed plan will pay for itself many times over.

There are many ways to create a strategy, but here are a few tried-and-proven principles that you might want to try.

1. Define your long-term objectives. What exactly do you hope to achieve? Spell each one out on paper in concrete, concise terms. For the greatest chance of success, narrow your focus to one or two primary objectives. You can take on more or diversify later, as resources permit.

2. Set short-term goals to reach your long-term objectives. In order to reach your long-term objectives, you will need steppingstones along the way. These should be smaller goals that together will get you to the final destination of your long-term objectives. They should be detailed and specific, concrete and measurable. If a goal isn't something that you'll be able to tick off as done, if it can't be quantified, then it's not specific enough.

Breaking down your goals into bite-sized pieces is crucial. The simpler and easier your goals are to reach, the better, because you'll see more immediate progress. It's easy to overestimate and shoot too high when setting your goals. It's also wise to realize that reaching big objectives takes time. Having a number of smaller goals will help keep the motivation level high, because you'll see more tangible progress. And every time you tick off one of your smaller goals, you're that much closer to your long-term objective.

3. Identify any obstacles. Once you have determined your long-term objectives and your short-term goals, you should take a look at any obstacles, or cons, or things that might stand in the way of achieving the results you're after. If you are alerted to potential problems, you can head them off by proactively praying for potential solutions.

4. Formulate a strategy. Once you have determined your long-term objectives and the short-term goals, you need a plan that includes specific tasks that will help you reach each of your short-term goals. Your plan must be realistic. A lofty plan may look impressive, but if it's too complicated or difficult to implement, it will never get off the ground and therefore be ineffective.

Assign the specific tasks that will be involved. Determine who will be responsible for each step, when they should have it done by, and if it's possible to know at this stage, how it should be done. Accountability is vital to success, as otherwise there will be no follow-through and no progress.

5. Ask God for guidance. Once you've taken the preceding steps, ask God in prayer to confirm that you're going in the right direction, that you have chosen the right priorities, that you haven't overlooked anything crucial, and that your long-term objectives and your short-term goals are realistic. "A man's heart plans his way, but the Lord directs his steps."[1] "Lean not on your own understanding; in all your ways acknowledge Him, and He shall direct your paths."[2]

6. Document the plan. Unless you document the plan clearly, things will be forgotten and left undone, and you might as well not have gone to all the trouble of having created the plan in the first place. Good documentation is vital for follow-through, accountability, and gauging progress.

7. Execute! The most common pitfall of planning is failing to implement the plan. People invest in creating a great plan, and they have the best intentions in the world for carrying it out. But things come up, life is busy, and they don't follow through.

8. Monitor your progress. Set in place a means to monitor progress at regular intervals. Make sure that tasks are getting done when they're supposed to and that progress is being made toward reaching your short-term goals. If you don't stop regularly to check your "map" and see where you are, you're less likely to stay on the road to success.

9. Expect the unexpected. Be flexible. Things rarely happen exactly as we imagine they will. As you monitor your progress, be prepared for new factors and adapt accordingly. If something comes up that makes it impossible to carry out a task as you had hoped, look around for alternatives. If something isn't working, change it. Generally follow your plan, but don't set it in stone.

10. Keep it simple. Guard against additions or complications that would overload the time and resources you've allocated to reaching a particular goal. When you first plan something, it often looks simple enough. But as you go along, the project grows—either because you keep adding new ideas, or because things are just more complicated than you thought—and usually some of both. Recognize when your plan is becoming overloaded, and determine what is necessary and what is not. Be willing to cut the frills and scale back on aspects that are just too costly in terms of resources.

11. Celebrate your successes, the milestones along the way. Don't wait till you reach your long-term objectives. Celebrating the completion of short-term goals generates satisfaction and excitement.

Peter Amsterdam ■

[1] Proverbs 16:9

[2] Proverbs 3:5–6

Blank spaces
A SPIRITUAL EXERCISE

THEN THEY ARE GLAD BECAUSE THEY ARE QUIET;
SO HE GUIDES THEM TO THEIR DESIRED HAVEN.
Psalm 107:30

It has been said that when it comes to helping those we care about, prayer is not the least we can do, but the most. The Bible promises, "This is the confidence that we have in [God], that if we ask anything according to His will, He hears us. And if we know that He hears us, whatever we ask, we know that we have the petitions that we have asked of Him."[1] That's a lot of power!

There are many times during the day when our thoughts wander aimlessly, and those thoughts usually involve others—friends, family, colleagues, or those we've crossed paths with or heard about in the news. Perhaps you are stuck in traffic, or you have your hands in dishwater, or are taking a walk, or are waiting to fall asleep at night. When you find yourself in one of these blank spots and someone springs to mind, instead of only thinking about that person, turn your thoughts into a prayer. Instead of wondering how your nephew is doing in school, pray for him to excel and be happy. Instead of wondering if your mother is recovering from the flu, pray for her healing. Instead of worrying about your friend who just lost his job, pray for him to not be discouraged and to find a new one.

By making a conscious effort to direct your thoughts to God and ask for His help, you will not only be giving a great gift to those you care about, but you're likely to find greater peace of mind yourself. The more situations you ask God to take care of, the less you will have to worry about. "Cast all your anxieties on Him, for He cares about you."[2]

Abi May ■

[1] 1 John 5:14–15

[2] 1 Peter 5:7 (RSV)

Be an icon

The Greek word translated "image" in most English versions of the Bible is eikon, from which we get the word "icon." It is used in the Bible both literally (e.g., Matthew 22:20, where Jesus asked whose image was on the Roman coin), and figuratively (e.g., Colossians 1:15 and Hebrews 1:3, in which the apostle Paul says that Jesus is the express image of the invisible God). The Septuagint, which was the first standard translation of the Hebrew Old Testament into Greek, called Adam the "eikon of God."

The sculptures, paintings, and carvings in orthodox churches are called icons—the anglicized rendering of eikones. So are people who are greatly admired or considered so good at what they do—entertainers, sports stars, entrepreneurs, etc.—that they have practically become synonymous with their area of expertise. No sooner were computer screens invented, it seems, than they began to get cluttered with little pictures that are called icons. Some have even taken on a life of their own, like the yellow smiley face and its dramatic derivatives, which are called emoticons.

Some people also use the word "icon" to explain the Christian's role in the world. We are to strive to be images of Christ by doing as He did, or would do today. That's not a bad idea. If we can apply that to our fellow believers—if we can see them as images of the Lord—it engenders brotherly love and respect. Mother Teresa took that concept a step further. "I see Jesus in every human being," she said. "I say to myself, 'This is hungry Jesus, I must feed him. This is sick Jesus. This one has leprosy or gangrene; I must wash him and tend to him. I serve because I love Jesus.'"

Few of us will ever attain to the level of selfless love that Mother Teresa came to symbolize, but we can and should strive to be more like Jesus. We do that by spending time with Jesus, getting to know Him and His Word, and practicing what He preached and lived. "We all, with unveiled face, beholding as in a mirror the glory of the Lord, are being transformed into the same image from glory to glory, just as by the Spirit of the Lord."[1]

Richard Johnston ∎

[1] 2 Corinthians 3:18

I, not events, have the power to make me happy or unhappy today. I can choose which it shall be. Yesterday is dead, tomorrow hasn't arrived yet. I have just one day, today, and I'm going to be happy in it.

Groucho Marx

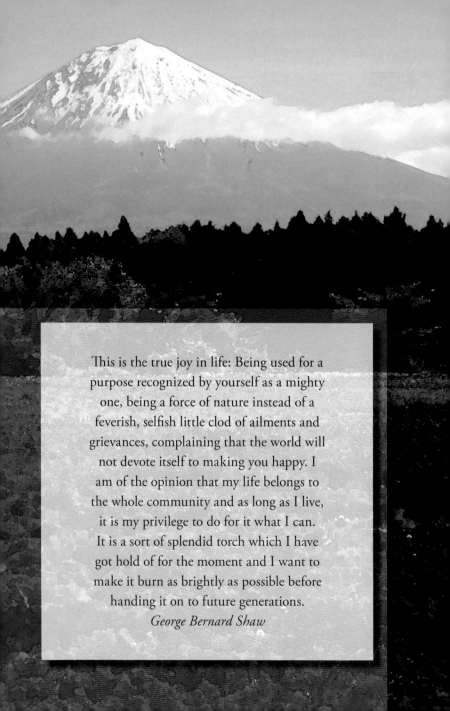

This is the true joy in life: Being used for a
purpose recognized by yourself as a mighty
one, being a force of nature instead of a
feverish, selfish little clod of ailments and
grievances, complaining that the world will
not devote itself to making you happy. I
am of the opinion that my life belongs to
the whole community and as long as I live,
it is my privilege to do for it what I can.
It is a sort of splendid torch which I have
got hold of for the moment and I want to
make it burn as brightly as possible before
handing it on to future generations.

George Bernard Shaw

Shorter strides, faster progress

THE STEPS OF A GOOD MAN ARE ORDERED BY THE LORD,
AND HE DELIGHTS IN HIS WAY.
Psalm 37:23

A couple of years ago I started running for exercise, and I've tried
to be consistent with it. I quickly built up to longer distances and
durations than when I started, but then I hit a plateau and stayed
there for a year or more. I found it difficult to increase my endurance
beyond a certain point, and I found it particularly difficult to
increase my speed.

Then about a month ago I went for a run with a friend who's
been running for years and is in excellent shape, and I asked him to
critique my running.

"If you take shorter strides than you're taking now and let your
feet move more quickly," he advised, "you'll last longer and your
running speed will pick up."

That hadn't occurred to me before. I hadn't been trying to move
in any particular manner, but just let my body take me where and
how it would. When I started paying attention and focusing on
taking smaller steps, I found that I didn't really have to try to move
more quickly; it just happened. The change wasn't dramatic, but
enough for me to tell I was making progress.

A month later my running has definitely improved. My breathing is less labored, my energy level stays higher, and my speed is increasing. This morning I ran the same distance on the track where I made my discovery, and did so in considerably less time, even without consciously trying. Best of all, I didn't feel like I was straining, struggling, and short on breath. I felt relaxed and enjoyed it from start to finish. I felt that I could have just as easily kept running.

While praying one morning shortly after my discovery, it occurred to me that I should test the same principle in other areas of my life, particularly my work. I like to think of myself as a "get things done" person, but I have to admit that I have a problem with procrastinating. It's not that I'm lazy. I'm happy to work hard and put in the hours, and I relish few things more than completing a project. Yet I find myself habitually avoiding the initial dig into large or long-term jobs, often putting them off until I have to cram to meet a deadline.

Recently I figured out why I do that: I've always assumed that I needed to make progress on big projects in big strides. But Jesus helped me see that by applying my running principle to my work, with smaller steps I could maximize efficiency, move more quickly, cover the same distance in less time and with less effort, and not be so exhausted at the end.

I no longer wait until I can clear a seven-day block on my calendar before starting a seven-day project. If I have an hour or two today, I can use that time and make a start—a small stride. Then I can work on it a bit tomorrow—another small stride—and a bit more the next day and the next. Working that way, I find myself getting to the end of what initially seemed like a daunting project, even without having devoted huge blocks of time. And I don't feel like I've run a marathon. The job got done because I picked away at it with small steps. And as it's happening, I can breathe! I'm not desperately playing catch-up. I'm not struggling to get in the mileage. I'm learning that sometimes the best and most lasting improvement is made not in one dramatic move, but bit by bit and step by step. Shorter strides make for faster progress.

Jessie Richards ∎

FROM THE END OF THE EARTH I WILL CRY TO YOU,
WHEN MY HEART IS OVERWHELMED;
LEAD ME TO THE ROCK THAT IS HIGHER THAN I.
Psalm 61:2

The way Jesus works in our lives and the way He chooses to do things is often past our comprehension. It's mysterious and usually takes faith and patience, because His timetable is often different from ours. Living the Christian life requires faith and trust, because we're not the ones in control—Jesus is. We have to remind ourselves constantly that He knows best, that He does all things well, and that His priorities are often different and much more long-term and "big picture" than ours.

Maria Fontaine

Whatever change you want to make in your life is possible. It doesn't matter what you've been like or how long you've been that way. It doesn't even matter if something you're trying to change is a part of your personality, your inborn nature, or something you feel is unchangeable. Even if you don't think you can change, you can because I can change you. If I made the world and everything in it, don't you see that it's a small thing for Me to transform a single life into something new, something even better?

A message from Jesus received in prayer ∎

CHAPTER 7

Persistence and Patience

LET US NOT GROW WEARY WHILE DOING GOOD, FOR IN DUE
SEASON WE SHALL REAP IF WE DO NOT LOSE HEART.
Galatians 6:9

Patience is power; with time and patience
the mulberry leaf becomes silk.
Chinese proverb

By perseverance the snail reached the ark.
Charles Haddon Spurgeon

They used to build bridges by first flying a kite from one side of the river or gorge to the other. Someone on the opposite side caught the kite and tied a little thicker, stronger string to the end of the kite string, and the men who had sent the kite over pulled the new, thicker string back across. The teams on each side kept repeating the process, next with an even stronger string, then a cord, then a thin rope, then a thicker rope, and so on. Eventually they could pull a small steel cable across, then a heavier one, until finally they had a cable across the expanse that was strong enough to support them and their tools and materials.—And it all started with one tiny kite string!

That's how habits are formed, both good and bad. Add a thread every day, and before long you can't break it. Start developing a good habit by taking the first step, however small, in the right direction. Then keep at it until you've built up a routine that can't easily be broken.

Peter Amsterdam ∎

Burden or blessing?

WHAT MAN IS THERE AMONG YOU WHO, IF HIS SON ASKS
FOR BREAD, WILL GIVE HIM A STONE? OR IF HE ASKS FOR A FISH,
WILL HE GIVE HIM A SERPENT? IF YOU THEN, BEING EVIL, KNOW
HOW TO GIVE GOOD GIFTS TO YOUR CHILDREN, HOW MUCH
MORE WILL YOUR FATHER WHO IS IN HEAVEN GIVE
GOOD THINGS TO THOSE WHO ASK HIM!
Matthew 7:9–11

Many things that seem to us to be curses are in fact gifts from God, oddly packaged.

The story is told of a woman who loved Jesus very much and wanted nothing more than to please Him. "I'll gladly do whatever You ask," she promised, hoping secretly for some noble and noticed place of service.

To her dismay He handed her a heavy, rough burlap sack and asked her to carry it as they walked through life together. She was curious about the contents of the sack, but it was tied closed with a strong cord and so many intricate knots that clearly it was not meant to be opened just yet.

As they started on their way, the woman sank down under the weight of her burden. "It's too heavy!" she protested.

"My strength is made perfect in your weakness,[1] and I will always be at your side," Jesus reassured her. "When the way gets steep or you feel faint, lean on Me."

So they walked on together, and it was just as Jesus had said. Sometimes the woman stopped and told Him that the weight was too much for her to bear, and so they bore it together.

By and by they arrived at their destination. The woman set her bundle down at Jesus' feet and heaved a sigh of relief. Her burden-bearing days were over.

"Let's see what's inside," Jesus said with a twinkle in His eye. With one stroke of His hand the knots were undone, the sack fell open, and the contents spilled out.

"The riches of heaven!" the woman exclaimed as her eyes feasted on treasures of unearthly beauty.

"This is your eternal reward—My gift in appreciation for all you have been through," Jesus explained.

Astonishment turned to tears of joy. The woman fell at Jesus' feet and said, "Oh Lord, forgive me! I misunderstood all these years. If I had only trusted You and not doubted and questioned! If only I had understood what was inside the sack, it would have been a joy to carry. I never should have grumbled or complained!"

You may look around and see others whose burdens appear to be much lighter than your own, and you may wish you could trade places. But if God were to grant you your wish, you would find that their burden would be even heavier and harder for you to carry than your own, for it was not meant for you. Each burden is tailor-made for its bearer, and is fashioned with the greatest of love and care. God knows exactly what's best for you. Trust Him.

Shannon Shayler ∎

[1] 2 Corinthians 12:9

Results and roses

So we built the wall, and the entire wall was
joined together up to half its height, for
the people had a mind to work.
Nehemiah 4:6

The man who wants a garden fair,
Or small or very big,
With flowers growing here and there,
Must bend his back and dig.

The things are mighty few on earth
That wishes can attain.
Whate'er we want of any worth
We've got to work to gain.

It matters not what goal you seek
Its secret here reposes:
You've got to dig from week to week
To get results or roses.
Edgar Guest ■

> AS LONG AS HE SOUGHT THE LORD, GOD MADE HIM PROSPER.
> *2 Chronicles 26:5*

It's difficult when we feel we're not making progress in the areas we know we need to improve in. As much as we try and as many resolutions as we make, we sometimes can't seem to break bad habits or form new good ones. That can become so frustrating and disappointing that we eventually lose faith that we can change. Because we've tried before and failed, we feel we might as well give up.

Though you may sometimes feel that way, the change you desire is possible. You are God's creation, and like the loving Father He is, He's very interested in every aspect of your life. He's ready, willing, and able to give you what you need to be truly happy, make progress, and live up to your full potential. So if you're willing to let God help you, then you'll get the results you're looking for. All He needs is your cooperation and for you to put forth effort in the right direction. If you'll do what you can do, then He will do the rest.

Casey Parker ■

My riches are yours

The secret to obtaining both spiritual riches and material supply is actually quite simple: Realize what vast resources are at My disposal.

My Word contains hundreds of promises that are yours to claim. As you read, absorb, and claim them, you will see answers to your prayers that will thrill your soul and cause your faith to grow. And as you continue to read and absorb and claim, I will continue to answer and inspire and provide. Together we will create an unbeatable, unbreakable cycle of success.

That is not to say that your faith will never ebb or that you will never again go through difficult times. As long as you are in this present world you will experience good times and hard times. Problems are a necessary part of life, but your connection with Me and your faith in My love and promises can make all the difference in the world!

A message from Jesus received in prayer ■

Progress—one step at a time

Ask God to help you set goals and arrive at the best plan for achieving them.

> Cause me to know the way in which I should walk,
> For I lift up my soul to You.
> *Psalm 143:8*

> A man's heart plans his way,
> But the LORD directs his steps.
> *Proverbs 16:9*

Be conscientious; do what you can.

> The soul of a lazy man desires, and has nothing;
> But the soul of the diligent shall be made rich.
> *Proverbs 13:4*

> The plans of the diligent lead surely to plenty,
> But those of everyone who is hasty, surely to poverty.
> *Proverbs 21:5*

A faithful man will abound with blessings,
But he who hastens to be rich will not go unpunished.
Proverbs 28:20

See then that you walk circumspectly, not as fools but as wise,
redeeming the time, because the days are evil.
Ephesians 5:15–16

Thank God for His help, even if it isn't immediately evident.

Enter into His gates with thanksgiving,
And into His courts with praise.
Be thankful to Him, and bless His name.
Psalm 100:4

But thanks be to God, who gives us the victory
through our Lord Jesus Christ.
1 Corinthians 15:57

Be anxious for nothing, but in everything by prayer
and supplication, with thanksgiving, let your
requests be made known to God.
Philippians 4:6

Trust God for the future.

Therefore do not worry, saying, "What shall we eat?" or "What shall we drink?" or "What shall we wear?" Therefore do not worry about tomorrow, for tomorrow will worry about its own things. Sufficient for the day is its own trouble.
Matthew 6:31,34

Being confident of this very thing, that He who has begun a good work in you will complete it until the day of Jesus Christ;
Philippians 1:6

Have patience for the desired outcome.

By your patience possess your souls.
Luke 21:19

But let patience have its perfect work, that you may be perfect and complete, lacking nothing.
James 1:4 ■

LET US RUN WITH ENDURANCE THE RACE THAT IS SET BEFORE
US, LOOKING UNTO JESUS, THE AUTHOR
AND FINISHER OF OUR FAITH.
Hebrews 12:1-2

A teacher took her primary school students to the assembly hall for a lesson with a difference. Standing at the foot of the steps leading up to the stage, she asked, "Is anybody good at jumping?"

Quite a few young hands shot up.

"Well," she continued, "could any of you jump from the floor here up onto the stage?"

No hands went up this time.

"I can," said the teacher, "and I'll show you how." Beginning at the foot of the steps leading up to the stage, she hopped onto the first step. From there she hopped onto the second, and so on until she reached the top.

Many things can only be accomplished little by little, step by step. When a task looks daunting or the way ahead too steep, just take it one step at a time.

Abi May ■

Anxiety, sickness, suffering,
or danger […] may make us
pause, and cause the spirit to
waver, and the soul to sink; but
let this only be for a moment.
All these are nothing when
compared with the glory which
shall be revealed in and for us.
David Livingstone

During any time of change, it's vital to hold on to God's unfailing, all-knowing love. Remind yourself that He is in control and that He has your best interests at heart. No matter what's happened in the past or what may happen in the future, God is your constant.

He is your heavenly shepherd, and He will not lead you astray or into harm's way. His love for you will never diminish. His strength and power will never wane.

Maria Fontaine

Got potential?

IF WE HOPE FOR THAT WE SEE NOT, THEN DO WE WITH
PATIENCE WAIT FOR IT.
Romans 8:25

What can you realistically expect to be or accomplish? That depends in part on how you define "realistic." Nobody knows what we're capable of better than God, and often His definition of "realistic" is "potential."

He knows our limits—"He knows our frame; He remembers that we are dust"[1]—but He also sees our hearts and continually looks at us from the viewpoint of what we can become.

God expects us to do what we can, but He doesn't expect us to be perfect. He knows we'll never be perfect, and if we're smart we'll realize that it's foolish for us to try or pretend to be. We have to do our part, but our part isn't to be perfect—and that's the beauty of God's plan!

Once we receive Jesus as our Savior, He lives in us. And if we will remember that we're weak and imperfect and nothing, really, without Him,[2] He can come through and be our everything. "We have this treasure in earthen vessels, that the excellence of the power may be of God and not of us."[3] His strength is made perfect in our weakness.[4]

God loves to do amazing, extraordinary things through some of the most unlikely, imperfect people who find themselves in the most seemingly impossible situations. He does that to show us what He can do. It's never about how good or strong we are. It's about God and His goodness and power.

With God nothing is impossible, and He knows that no matter what has happened in the past or what our current weaknesses or lacks may be, we can change; He can make us better. We must learn to see ourselves through the eyes of faith, through the perspective of what we can become, what God's power can transform us into, what Jesus can be in us.

So what if you aren't perfect! Who is? You can still be a great success in life if you let the Spirit of God work in you and through you. His Spirit will fill in the gaps of the little problems and imperfections. God doesn't need perfection from us to work His wonders.

Make room for God to work by not looking at your shortcomings and imperfections, but rather by looking to Him to help you reach your full potential as you do your part and hold Him to the promises He has made to you in His Word.

Peter Amsterdam ■

¹ Psalm 103:14

² John 15:5

³ 2 Corinthians 4:7

⁴ 2 Corinthians 12:9

CHAPTER 8

People: Love

IF YOU WANT OTHERS TO BE HAPPY, PRACTICE COMPASSION.
IF YOU WANT TO BE HAPPY, PRACTICE COMPASSION.
The Dalai Lama

The door to happiness swings outward.
Søren Kierkegaard

Then one of them, a lawyer, asked Him a question,
testing Him, and saying,
"Teacher, which is the great commandment in the law?"
Jesus said to him, "'You shall love the Lord your God with all
your heart, with all your soul, and with all your mind.' This
is the first and great commandment. And the second is like
it: 'You shall love your neighbor as yourself.' On these two
commandments hang all the Law and the Prophets."
Matthew 22:37–40

Live to love, love to give

Do all the good you can,
By all the means you can,
In all the ways you can,
In all the places you can,
At all the times you can,
To all the people you can,
As long as ever you can.
Attributed to John Wesley

There is a wonderful law of nature that the three things we
crave most in life—happiness, freedom, and peace of mind—
are always attained by giving them to someone else.
Peyton Conway March

We make a living by what we get,
but we make a life by what we give.
Sir Winston Churchill

It is every man's obligation to put back into the world
at least the equivalent of what he takes out of it.
Albert Einstein

No person was ever honored for what he received.
He was honored for what he gave.
Calvin Coolidge ■

Walk a mile in his shoes

LET US NOT LOVE IN WORD OR IN TONGUE,
BUT IN DEED AND IN TRUTH.

1 John 3:18

"Never judge a man until you've walked a mile in his shoes." If there was anyone who knew all about that, it was probably Mother Teresa. After having lived among the poorest of the poor in India for nearly 30 years (and she would continue to do so for nearly 20 more), she was awarded the 1979 Nobel Peace Prize. She began her acceptance speech with the words, "Life is life." She went on to explain that all human beings are special and of great worth, no matter who they are, and that only when we have learned to respect that fact can we begin to help them improve their lives.

Most people would be happy to walk a mile in a pair of plush designer shoes or top-of-the-line athletic shoes, but how many would want to step into a poor laborer's shoes? When I was living in Uganda, East Africa, I found a discarded pair of shoes that became to me a symbol of Africa and its sweet-spirited but struggling people. It was apparent from the cement splatters that their last owner had been a construction worker. Like many others I observed there, he no doubt worked long days in sweltering heat with no protection against the sun and had only a couple of sticks of raw sugar cane for lunch. He had worn those shoes until the holes in the soles had gotten so big that the shoes no longer served their purpose. When there was no point in wearing them one more day, he left them for me to find. It wasn't his intention, of course, but those shoes put my own petty problems into perspective.

There wasn't any question in my mind when, some time later, a young man knocked at my door, asking for help. He had won a scholarship to a boarding school, but there was one requirement he couldn't fulfill—he didn't have any shoes. He asked if I had an extra pair I could give him. The ones I was wearing at the time fit him quite nicely, and that was that.

No, one simple act of kindness didn't make me a saint on the level of Mother Teresa, but I do believe that in that moment I experienced a touch of what motivated her all those years: "The love of Christ compels us."[1]

Curtis Peter van Gorder ∎

[1] 2 Corinthians 5:14

A stray dog moved into the Smiths' neighborhood the same day the Joneses moved in next door, and the dog immediately began to wreak havoc, scrounging in trashcans and tearing up flowerbeds in both yards. The Smiths were irked that the Joneses had brought such a nuisance into the neighborhood, and the Joneses found it inexcusable that the Smiths made no attempt to control their dog. For several weeks neither couple said anything to the other, while bad feelings festered on both sides. Finally Ms. Smith could stand no more and gave Ms. Jones a piece of her mind. "Oh," Ms. Jones replied, "we thought it was your dog!"

Often the things that sour relationships are like that dog—more a matter of misunderstandings or small irritations that get blown out of proportion than actual wrongdoing on anyone's part. Usually all it takes to set things right is better communication, but someone has to make the first move, and that's not always easy. Both parties, convinced that they're right or unwilling to admit that they're not, lock themselves into their positions. Barriers go up. Relationships go bad. Everyone suffers.

Where can we find the humility to admit we've been in the wrong, or the love and grace to forgive and forget when we've been wronged? Where can we find the wisdom to turn a no-win situation into a win-win situation, the strength to buck our stubborn nature, or the courage to make the first move? All these and more are at our disposal anytime, whatever we need, when we need it, in unlimited supply, free of charge. "Every good and every perfect gift is from above."[1] "Ask, and it will be given to you."[2] Like all of the other best things in life, the most successful relationships begin with the ultimate relationship—heart to heart communion with "the living God, who gives us richly all things to enjoy."[3]

Keith Phillips ■

[1] James 1:17 (NIV)

[2] Matthew 7:7

[3] 1 Timothy 6:17

Build bridges not walls

LET US LOVE ONE ANOTHER, FOR LOVE IS OF GOD; AND
EVERYONE WHO LOVES IS BORN OF GOD AND KNOWS GOD.

1 John 4:7

It's been said that people are lonely because they build walls instead of bridges. How true!

Most people tend to be a little selfish. It's human nature to "look out for number one," to put your own needs and desires before the needs of others. It's easy enough to get caught up in your own life and problems, but when you do that, you're creating a bigger problem by closing yourself off to many wonderful things in life and many wonderful people.

When you build bridges by reaching out to and connecting with others, it may add a few problems and complications, but it's worth the trouble because it also brings warmth, friendship, love, and other blessings into your life. It is a matter of give and take, and it does

require some effort, patience, and perseverance. The bridge doesn't build itself, and sometimes others aren't so keen at first to see you building in their direction. But if everyone got stuck in the me-first mentality and built nothing but walls, the world would be a terribly lonely place.

Building a bridge begins with a prayer for love and understanding and for Me to help you change in other areas as needed. When you begin to think in terms of what others want and need, the framework is in place. Then that bridge grows a little stronger each time you give of yourself to that hard-to-reach person. It might take a little courage to cross that bridge the first time, when you're not sure how well it's going to hold or how you'll be received on the other side, but you'll be glad you did. I will bless every unselfish act, and honor every step you take to reach out to another.

A message from Jesus received in prayer ■

1 Corinthians 13

Jesus gave us the key to happiness and harmony when He said, "Love your neighbor as yourself."[1] What exactly does that mean, in practical, everyday terms? One of the best explanations ever given is found in the Bible's "love chapter," 1 Corinthians 13. Times and terms have changed, but the underlying principles are as true as ever. Here's how the apostle Paul might have put it if he were writing to us today.

1. Though I can speak five languages and talk intelligently on dozens of subjects, if I don't have enough love to keep from gossiping or putting down others, I'm not just making so much useless noise, I'm being downright destructive.

2. And though I read the Bible regularly and even know parts of it by heart, and though I pray daily and have a lot of faith and other spiritual gifts, if I don't have enough love to sometimes sacrifice some of my personal desires for others' sakes, then all of my "spirituality" amounts to nothing.

3. And though I work two jobs to provide for my family, and though I give to charity and volunteer for every community project that comes up, if I don't show love and kindness to those I live and work with, all my hard work and self-sacrifice are worthless.

4. Love has a long, hard, frustrating day at the office, yet doesn't get snappy and short tempered. Love is happy for the other guy when he gets all the breaks. Love doesn't have to drive the flashiest car, live in the biggest house, or have all the latest gadgets. Love doesn't always have to be the boss or have the last word.

5. Love isn't rude or crude, isn't selfish, and doesn't gripe or pressure others to get what it wants. Love is too busy being concerned about the needs of others to spend much time worrying about its own. Love doesn't freak out when things don't go its way. Love is quick to believe the best about people and slow to believe the rest.

6. Love hates to hear gossip and instead wants only to talk about others' good qualities and the good that they've done. Love knows that what it listens to, watches, or reads will affect its attitudes and actions and thereby have an effect on others, so it's careful about how it spends its time.

7. Love is flexible, takes things in stride, and can handle whatever comes its way. Love is always ready to give others the benefit of the doubt and looks for the best in them. Love wants to see others reach their full potential and does all it can to make that happen. Love never runs out of patience, even with those who are slow to get with the program or do their share. Love doesn't keep looking at its watch when others are talking.

8. Love never fails. I fail others, and others can fail me. We all can be mistaken, misguided, or confused at times. Our words and deeds often fall short, and our bright ideas don't always play out the way we want or expect them to.

9. We're frail, fallible, and often foolish, and our understanding of the world we live in, not to mention the world to come, is only partial at best.

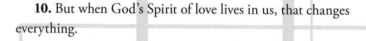

10. But when God's Spirit of love lives in us, that changes everything.

11. We're really just children when it comes to practicing real love, but God can help us outgrow our childish ways.

12. Without Him we're clueless when it comes to love and the other things that matter most in life, but when we live in His kingdom—the kingdom of heaven that Jesus said is even now within us—we can see things as He does, get our priorities straight, pull out the stops, and live and love to the full.

13. There are lots of nice things in life and lots of good things, but none are as good or as important as love!

Adapted from Maria Fontaine by Josie Clark ■

---

[1] Matthew 22:39

Appreciation
A SPIRITUAL EXERCISE

Jesus taught "Do to others as you would have them do to you."[1] There are many ways to put this Golden Rule into practice; appreciation is one.

Think for a moment about your family, friends, colleagues, and acquaintances. Doesn't it make your day when one of them says or does something to show they appreciate you?

Everyone benefits from appreciation. Here's an exercise to strengthen your appreciation skills.

Pick three people that you interact with daily, and make it a goal to show appreciation to each of them at least once today. Be on the lookout for things that you genuinely admire about them or can thank or commend them for, and say or do something that tells them so. Take a moment at the end of the day to reflect on how it went. Did you meet your goal? What effect did it have on the recipients?

Repeat the exercise every day for a week, targeting some of the same people and some new ones as the week progresses. Make an effort to not choose only those people you like most or feel closest to. Even the most difficult people to get along with have some good qualities.

Showing appreciation will not only give the recipient a lift, it will also improve your own outlook by helping you view those around you more positively. It seems to be human nature to notice the bad more easily than the good, and it's often relatively minor things that sour our relations, such as idiosyncrasies that we find irritating. By making a conscious effort to look for things to appreciate in others, focusing on the good will override human nature and make you a more positive person.

Appreciation is contagious. It may not happen overnight, but in time it will nearly always bring about a remarkable change in any home, workplace, or circle of friends.

Abi May ■

---

[1] Luke 6:31 (NIV)

Life is a series of situations
and decisions. When we
focus on the uncertainties,
we become paralyzed. But
when we take our problems
to God and look to Him in
our decision making, His
assurances propel us in the
right direction.
Ross Conn

God wants what's best for us, but
often the means to that end involves
taking us through both triumphs
and trials, joy and pain. From our
perspective, a particular situation or
event may not seem good, but from
God's perspective, it's what He wants
for us because He knows it will further
His plan. He sees farther than we do,
and His plans are better and more
complete than ours.

Alex Peterson

Then the King will say to those on His right hand,
"Come, you blessed of My Father, inherit the kingdom
prepared for you from the foundation of the world: for I was
hungry and you gave Me food; I was thirsty and you gave Me
drink; I was a stranger and you took Me in; I was naked and
you clothed Me; I was sick and you visited Me; I was in prison
and you came to Me. … Assuredly, I say to you, inasmuch
as you did it to one of the least of these
My brethren, you did it to Me."
Matthew 25:34–36,40

You learn to speak by speaking, to study by studying, to run
by running, to work by working; and just so, you learn to love
by loving. All those who think to learn in any
other way deceive themselves.
Francis de Sales

Remember Rubik's Cube, the intriguing puzzle? Brian
Cramer likened love to a Rubik's Cube, explaining, "There are
countless numbers of wrong twists and turns, but when
you get it right, it looks perfect no matter
what way you look at it."
Abi May ■

CHAPTER 9

Priorities

LET US HEAR THE CONCLUSION OF THE WHOLE MATTER:
FEAR GOD AND KEEP HIS COMMANDMENTS,
FOR THIS IS MAN'S ALL.
Ecclesiastes 12:13

Do not lay up for yourselves treasures on earth, where moth
and rust destroy and where thieves break in and steal; but lay
up for yourselves treasures in heaven, where neither moth nor
rust destroys and where thieves do not break in
and steal. For where your treasure is,
there your heart will be also.
Matthew 6:19–21

What counts

NOW ABIDE FAITH, HOPE, LOVE, THESE THREE;
BUT THE GREATEST OF THESE IS LOVE.
1 Corinthians 13:13

A quote hanging in Albert Einstein's office read: "Not everything that counts can be counted, and not everything that can be counted counts." In other words, a lot of the things you do in a day or week can't be "counted"—they're not things that you can tick off of your to-do list—and yet they are vital, defining moments.

We must be sure to always keep in the forefront of our minds that love is the most important thing. If we don't have love, all of our ticked-off to-dos, all of our great accomplishments, will be of no benefit.

The number one priority is and always should be love! If you can go to bed at night knowing that you have shown love, then you can rest well, knowing that you've accomplished something truly great.

Maria Fontaine ∎

Building a life

THEREFORE WHOEVER HEARS THESE SAYINGS OF MINE, AND
DOES THEM, I WILL LIKEN HIM TO A WISE MAN WHO BUILT HIS
HOUSE ON THE ROCK: AND THE RAIN DESCENDED, THE FLOODS
CAME, AND THE WINDS BLEW AND BEAT ON THAT HOUSE; AND
IT DID NOT FALL, FOR IT WAS FOUNDED ON THE ROCK.

Matthew 7:24–25

An elderly carpenter was ready to retire, and he told his boss of his plans to leave and live a more leisurely life with his wife. He would miss the paycheck, but he needed to retire. They could get by.

The contractor was sorry to see such a good worker go, and he asked the carpenter to build just one more house as a personal favor.

The carpenter said yes, but in time it was easy to see that his heart was not in his work. He resorted to shoddy workmanship and used inferior materials. It was an unfortunate way to end a dedicated career.

When the carpenter finished his work, the employer came to inspect the house. He handed the front-door key to the carpenter. "This is your house," he said. "It is my gift to you."

The carpenter was shocked! What a shame! If he had only known he was building his own house, he would have done it all so differently.

So it is with us. We build our lives, a day at a time, often putting less than our best into the building. Then with a shock we realize we have to live in the house we have built.

If we could do it over, we'd do it much differently. But we cannot go back.

You are the carpenter of your life. Each day you hammer a nail, place a board, or erect a wall. Your attitudes and the choices you make today build your "house" for tomorrow. Build wisely!

Author unknown ■

ABIDE IN ME, AND I IN YOU.
John 15:4

Abide in Me and let Me abide in you continually. Talk to Me, sing to Me, converse with Me, listen to Me, commune with Me. That sounds good, you may think, but it also sounds very spiritual, and you wonder if you can do it. But in reality it's a very practical matter with very practical benefits. It's also not hard once you get in the habit. You think all day long, don't you? Don't you always have thoughts running through your mind—how to do this or that, where to go when, what to say next, and so on? You talk to yourself continually. Well, talk to Me instead. Why talk to yourself when you can talk to Me and get My help?

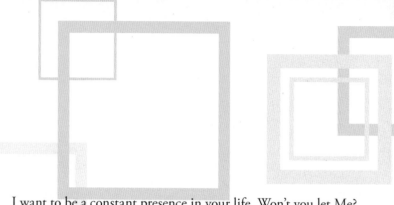

I want to be a constant presence in your life. Won't you let Me? Won't you talk to Me more as you go about your business, sharing your thoughts and desires with Me? I want to share My thoughts and heart with you too, to develop bonds of love and fellowship and to be that constant presence, that constant companion, because I love you.

As you give Me more room in your thoughts, you will take on more of My mind, My attitudes, My thoughts. Then I will be able to get through to you easier and better guide your actions. I will be able to give you the right perspective on your work, your relations with others, yourself, and the world around you. I will be able to remind you of things to do, give you new ideas or new ways of doing things, and provide the answers you need. Come to Me in quietness and trust, and you will find the strength and power you need. Draw close to Me and I will draw close to you. That's a promise!

A message from Jesus received in prayer ■

Making resolutions realities

1. Make a list of your goals and select the top three to five that are the most important to you. Pray for God's guidance in the process. He knows best.

2. Be realistic. Reaching for a goal should stretch you, but it should also be doable. Decide on a reasonable time frame for reaching each goal.

3. Don't try to do everything at once. Focus on your top goal for a set period of time. Then move to goal number two, while maintaining the progress made toward reaching the first one, and so on.

4. Pray. Prayer brings into play the spiritual help you need to reach your goals.

5. Work with God. Change involves overcoming past thought and behavioral patterns. This is never easy, but change for the better is possible if you ask God to help and follow His lead. "With God nothing will be impossible."[1]

6. Chart your progress. Keep track of how far you've come, using a journal or chart. Keeping records and reviewing them periodically can also help you to identify weak spots.

7. Get help from others. Share your plan with a friend and ask for his or her help. Being accountable to someone will give you added incentive to stick to your resolutions even when it's tough.

8. Don't be discouraged by your mistakes. You will have some setbacks and "off" days. Take these lows as a reminder that you can't do it on your own. Draw closer to God and depend more on His help. Tomorrow is a fresh chance to do better!

9. Be in it for the long haul. If you are truly serious about making a change, you will be willing to see it through, no matter how long it takes.

10. Visualize victory. Periodically visualize what your life will be like once your goal is reached. Picture the advantages you will gain and how much happier, healthier, or more productive you will be.

11. Reward yourself for each goal you reach. The real reward will be the feeling of accomplishment and the benefits you'll experience from the change you've made, but having a physical treat attached to a specific goal can make it even more enjoyable.

Alex Peterson ■

¹ Luke 1:37

The rule of five

NOW THAT THE WORST IS OVER, WE'RE PLEASED WE CAN
REPORT THAT WE'VE COME OUT OF THIS WITH CONSCIENCE
AND FAITH INTACT, AND CAN FACE THE WORLD—AND EVEN
MORE IMPORTANTLY, FACE YOU WITH OUR HEADS HELD HIGH.
BUT IT WASN'T BY ANY FANCY FOOTWORK ON OUR PART. IT WAS
GOD WHO KEPT US FOCUSED ON HIM, UNCOMPROMISED.
2 Corinthians 1:12 (THE MESSAGE)

It never ceases to amaze me how much Jesus wants to be a part of our lives by giving us practical, tangible help. When I was discouraged about my inability to get organized, I took the problem to Jesus during my quiet time with Him. "There is no way that I will be able to meet my life goals with this serious state of disorganization," I told Him. "I try to change, but I need Your help, because without it I keep slipping into my old pattern of doing nothing because I cannot do everything. How can I overcome this problem?"

Faithful as always, He spoke to my heart with words of encouragement about how much He loves me, even though I'm not perfect and don't accomplish as much as I think I should. Any forward progress is better than nothing, He reminded me. He didn't design us to succeed every time, only to be able to move forward, to learn and progress, and through that process to eventually become all we can be.

Jesus then gave me a few pointers to help me to make progress in this area, including what I have come to call "the rule of five." The crux of my problem was that I had accumulated way too many things—clutter that led to a feeling of chaos. Some things I needed, some I had kept because I thought I might need them someday, and some were just plain junk.

Jesus didn't suggest that I embark on a huge reorganizing project that would have been very taxing and nearly impossible to follow through on, but rather that I start by trying to get rid of five unnecessary things each day. It could be as simple as putting a brochure that I'm through with into the recycle bin. I am also trying to pass on nice things that I will probably never use again, like that item of clothing that would fit if I were to lose some weight, but which would look great on a friend right now. You get the idea. I've been able to give lots of small gifts to friends, donate some other things to needy causes, and throw away the junk—and it has brought me back to the joys of simple, uncluttered living.

Of course some days I forget or don't have time, and I still have a lot of stuff to work through, but the rule of five has given me a plan that works and I no longer constantly feel like an organizational failure.

Lily Neve ■

The ground of a certain rich man yielded plentifully. And he thought within himself, saying, "What shall I do, since I have no room to store my crops?"

So he said, "I will do this: I will pull down my barns and build greater, and there I will store all my crops and my goods. And I will say to my soul, "Soul, you have many goods laid up for many years; take your ease; eat, drink, and be merry."

But God said to him, "Fool! This night your soul will be required of you; then whose will those things be which you have provided?"

So is he who lays up treasure for himself, and is not rich toward God.

Luke 12:16–21 ■

CHAPTER 10

Plunge and Plummet

BRETHREN, I DO NOT COUNT MYSELF TO HAVE APPREHENDED;
BUT ONE THING I DO, FORGETTING THOSE THINGS WHICH ARE
BEHIND AND REACHING FORWARD TO THOSE THINGS WHICH
ARE AHEAD, I PRESS TOWARD THE GOAL FOR THE PRIZE OF
THE UPWARD CALL OF GOD IN CHRIST JESUS.

Philippians 3:13–14

A story is told of an elderly woman who slipped and fell on a busy street. Several people quickly went to assist her, but she was already struggling to hoist herself up. "I'm all right," she assured them. "I always fall forwards, never backwards."

When we've "taken a fall," instead of dwelling on the mistake or hurt, we need to make it a fall forward by learning from it and looking to the future.

Abi May

If you feel that you have made mistakes, taken wrong turns, even failed miserably at this or that, you're in good company. Many of God's heroes in the Bible did those same things, but they learned from their mistakes. And God came to them, sitting in the midst of failed dreams or disappointed hopes, and gave them a new reason to live. That's what He can do when we give up on our own plans and projects and decide to try His. He gives us goals to help us grow and move in the right direction, and then He helps us attain them. Give Him your heart and life, and let Him give you all the good things He has planned for you.

Nana Williams

Don't let mistakes of the past blur your vision for the future. Focus on the good to come.

Maria Fontaine ■

This world is God's
workshop for
making men in.
Henry Ward Beecher

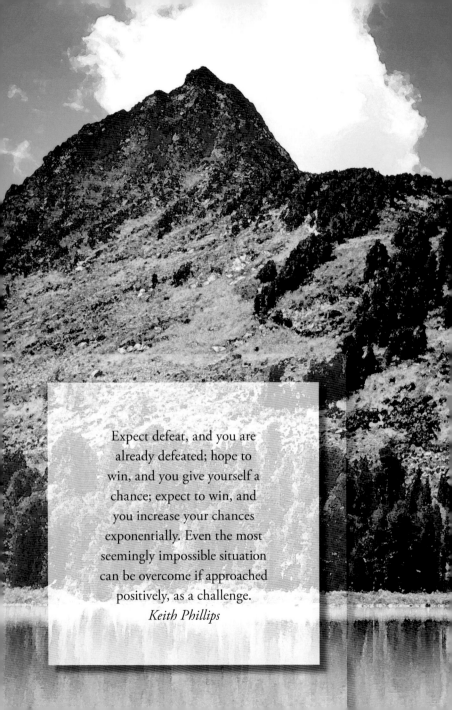

Expect defeat, and you are already defeated; hope to win, and you give yourself a chance; expect to win, and you increase your chances exponentially. Even the most seemingly impossible situation can be overcome if approached positively, as a challenge.

Keith Phillips

Falling together

WE KNOW THAT ALL THINGS WORK TOGETHER FOR GOOD TO
THOSE WHO LOVE GOD, TO THOSE WHO ARE THE
CALLED ACCORDING TO HIS PURPOSE.
Romans 8:28

"Everything is falling apart!" My outburst came one day after a
visit to the Kurasini Orphanage in Dar es Salaam, Tanzania, where
for the past two years our team of volunteers has been working
with the staff to raise the children's living standard. We had begun
by improving sanitation in the kitchen and dormitories, and some
progress had been made. But it seemed that there were always more
things that needed to get done. As the to-do list grew, so did the
list of needed materials and supplies. There was also the matter of
funding. How would we find enough sponsors to help meet all of
these needs?

We had been discussing the project over dinner when my mind
flashed back to the state of the nursery, and I felt overwhelmed with
frustration once again—hence my "Everything is falling apart!"
outburst.

One of my colleagues chuckled and reminded me of the dismal
condition the orphanage had been in the first time we saw it. Then he
listed the many changes that we had been able to make.

How foolish I felt! Yes, there was still much to do, but taking a few minutes to consider and appreciate how far we had come helped put things in perspective. Instead of feeling overwhelmed, I was overjoyed that so many changes had come to pass. Slowly but steadily, progress was being made.

Then I heard God's voice in my mind. "Who is ultimately in control?—I am! Who sees the situation more clearly and knows better how to fix it, you or Me?—I do! Who has come through for you every time you faced an 'impossible' situation in the past?—I have! The best thing you can do is to keep doing what you can day by day and keep praying. Trust Me, things will fall into place in My time!"

That was all I needed to hear. I felt a surge of energy and renewed determination. We would move forward with the things we could, taking one thing at a time and leaving the rest in God's hands. With God behind us, we could do this!

All of life is like that, of course. Many times the odds seem stacked against us, but if we'll stop and step back for a moment, we'll see once again that God is there to help. In His hands, things don't fall apart, they fall together.

Heidi Dansholm ∎

WHEN YOU PASS THROUGH THE WATERS, I WILL BE WITH YOU;
AND THROUGH THE RIVERS, THEY SHALL NOT OVERFLOW YOU.
Isaiah 43:2

Have you ever noticed how some people can stay afloat when engulfed in troubles and hardships, while others sink to the bottom? What sets the swimmers apart from the sinkers? From what I've seen, the biggest factor seems to be faith in God's love. When those who understand how much God loves them find themselves in over their heads, they know He won't let them drown. So, unlike those who don't have such faith, they don't wear themselves out struggling just to keep their heads above water—or worse, panic and go down all the quicker. Buoyed by their faith, the swimmers can concentrate their energy on getting to solid ground. If you feel more like a sinker than a swimmer, you can get ready for the next sink-or-swim situation by strengthening your faith in God's love.

Keith Phillips ■

Thank God for the good
A SPIRITUAL EXERCISE

REJOICE ALWAYS, PRAY WITHOUT CEASING, IN EVERYTHING
GIVE THANKS; FOR THIS IS THE WILL OF GOD
IN CHRIST JESUS FOR YOU.
1 Thessalonians 5:16–18

Recall a discouraging or adverse situation that you were involved in recently, and then think about the good things that came out of your misfortune, or may yet. Try to think of at least three things. (Don't give up too soon. If you can think of even one good result, more will probably follow.) Then thank God for the good.

For example, let's say you were driving on a deserted road when your car broke down in the middle of nowhere, and when you tried to phone for help, you discovered that the battery in your cell phone was dead. Your thanks to God might go something like this:

"Thank You for putting me in that situation because it reminded me that no matter how helpless I feel, I'm never truly helpless because I always have You. Thank You that even when I was stranded out

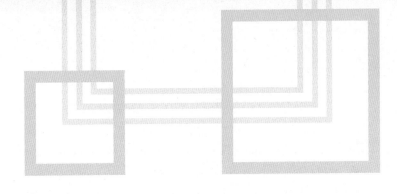

there with no help in sight and no phone to summon help, I was still able to contact You through prayer, and You came through for me. You sent a friendly stranger to help me, and even though it took awhile for him to get there, I made a new friend that I wouldn't have otherwise, and he got Your blessing for stopping to help, which he would have missed if the opportunity hadn't been there. Thank You for being, like the Bible says, 'a very present help in trouble.'"[1]

Practice this exercise each evening for the next week, and it will improve the way you react to troubles when they happen. Casting past troubles in a positive light will prepare you to approach future ones positively, and that is often half the battle won.

Abi May ■

[1] Psalm 46:1

At Gibeon the LORD appeared to Solomon in a dream by night; and God said, "Ask! What shall I give you?"

And Solomon said: "You have shown great mercy. ... Now, O LORD my God, You have made Your servant king ... but I am a little child; I do not know how to go out or come in. Therefore give to Your servant an understanding heart ... that I may discern between good and evil."

The speech pleased the LORD, that Solomon had asked this thing. Then God said to him:

"Because you have asked this thing, and have not asked long life for yourself, nor have asked riches for yourself ... but have asked for yourself understanding to discern justice, behold, I have done according to your words; see, I have given you a wise and understanding heart. ... And I have also given you what you have not asked: both riches and honor. ... So if you walk in My ways ... then I will lengthen your days."

1 Kings 3:5–14 ■

Resolutions

This year...
I'll take more time to laugh and smile,
To feel the wind upon my face,
To learn true wisdom from a child,
Give my soul the needed space,
To live life pure and clear...
...this year.

This year...
I'll learn to turn off my computer,
Interact with human beings,
Spend less time in online stupor,
More time learning, breathing, seeing
All that life holds dear...
...this year.

This year...
I will resolve to write that letter
That I have too long neglected,
Make an aching heart feel better,
Cheer a friend who feels dejected,
Bring someone some cheer...
...this year.

This year...
I'll not be hijacked by my deadlines,
Or imprisoned by ambitions.
Or let dismal, gloomy headlines
Dictate my heart's disposition.
I'll choose faith, not fear...
...this year.

This year...
I'll see the struggling flower beneath
The hard, frosty exterior
Of one who lets frustration seethe
Because they feel inferior.
I'll try to draw them near...
...this year.

This year...
No high-and-mighty resolutions
Fit for presidents and kings.
I'll start a quiet revolution,
Seek these simple loving things
Above wealth or career...
...this year.
Ian Bach ∎

Peace process

You will keep him in perfect peace,
Whose mind is stayed on You,
Because he trusts in You.
Isaiah 26:3

How can you find peace of mind and relief from discouragement? Simple. It is within My power to override the negative thoughts that drag you down, and that power is released through prayer and praise. When you turn whatever is bothering you over to Me and praise Me for taking care of it, your focus shifts from your problems to My power to solve them, and that puts your mind at ease. It's a three-step process:

First, hand your heart full of worries, problems, doubts, and fears over to Me.

Second, thank Me for taking care of them, even before you see the answers to your prayers.

Third, let the negative feelings dissolve and My peace fill your being.

How do you start praising, especially if you don't feel like it? Concentrate on Me and My power and goodness. This will probably take some effort on your part because your heart is weighed down with troubles, but once you start, I will carry you from there. I will fill you with peace and confidence. Your praises will also create a force field that will help shield you from further negativity. I can even give you the oomph you need to get started praising. Call out to Me in prayer, and I will answer. That's a promise!

A message from Jesus received in prayer ∎

Chapter 11

Pause for Prayer

LET ME HEAR WHAT GOD THE LORD WILL SPEAK, FOR HE WILL
SPEAK PEACE TO HIS PEOPLE, TO HIS SAINTS, TO THOSE WHO
TURN TO HIM IN THEIR HEARTS.
Psalm 85:8 (RSV)

If we have not quiet in our minds, outward comfort will do no
more for us than a golden slipper on a gouty foot.
John Bunyan

Peace comes not from the absence of trouble,
but from the presence of God.
Author unknown

Our daily lives can easily become filled with stress, pressure,
and confusion. But we can stop at any moment and slip
away into the presence of God's Spirit through prayer and
meditation, and there find peace and refreshing.
Maria Fontaine ■

If we want to get the best results, our time with Jesus in prayer and communication with Him can't just be quick and superficial, squeezed in here or there while our mind is still full of the business of the day. We have to take time to connect with Him, share our heart with Him, and let Him clear our mind and soothe our spirit.

Your time with Him is really the most important part of the day. If you get in the habit of taking that time first thing in the morning, His presence will be with you all day to guide and help you. It's a whole new mentality, really. Instead of trying to handle everything yourself and get through it all as quickly as you can, you will be letting Jesus do most of the work for you. You'll still have to play the part He shows you to play, but you'll have peace of mind that as you do your part, He will do the rest.

Maria Fontaine ■

Quality time

IF YOU ABIDE IN ME, AND MY WORDS ABIDE IN YOU, YOU WILL
ASK WHAT YOU DESIRE, AND IT SHALL BE DONE FOR YOU.

John 15:7

Many of us tend to pick up the pace when our workloads increase, and that leads to more stress. Taking time off to relax can help relieve the pressure, but time alone or with friends or family can't give us what Jesus can.

Hobbies can also be relaxing and fun, but if we're not careful, they can actually contribute to the problem by taking time away from the essentials, including the most essential—taking time with Jesus. That's a common mistake people make—filling every spare moment with more "busyness," when the Lord wants them to take that time with Him.

The surest way to complete and lasting renewal—in fact, the only way—is to spend time with Jesus. We need His love and strength and wisdom, and the only way we can get those is by spending time with Him.

But carving out time from your daily schedule is no guarantee that you're going to get closer to the Lord; it's what you do with that time that counts. You need to get still, empty your mind of the business of the day, and let the Lord fill you with positive, encouraging, strengthening, faith-building thoughts from His recorded and living Word.

Jesus said the requirement for a fruitful life is abiding in Him. "Abide in Me, and I in you."[1] That means staying connected with Him by taking time to read His Word and pray and listen to Him.

It's easy to let prayer become a formality, but one thing that can help you avoid that is to think of Jesus as the friend, counselor, and lover that He wants to be to you. As someone once said, "The more one loves Jesus, the more he delights to be with Jesus alone. Lovers love to be alone."

But He won't push you. He waits to see how much you are willing to abandon all other distractions in order to put Him first. If you have Him in first place, then you will see and feel His power and help in your life beyond what you ever imagined.

Peter Amsterdam ■

[1] John 15:4

"God finds ways to communicate with those who truly seek Him," best-selling Christian author Philip Yancey wrote, "especially when we lower the volume of the surrounding static." Nearly 300 years earlier, Isaac Newton made the same discovery, which he explained this way: "I can take my telescope and look millions of miles into space; but I can lay my telescope aside, go into my room and shut the door, and while in earnest prayer I see more of heaven and get closer to God than I can when assisted by all the telescopes and material agencies on earth."

The apostle Paul tells us, "We all, with unveiled face, beholding as in a mirror the glory of the Lord, are being transformed into the same image from glory to glory."[1] In other words, we take on His divine nature.

If that kind of quiet reflection can get that kind of results— direct communication with God and transformation from our lowly human state to godliness—then why don't we do it more often? Very often it's due to the "surrounding static." We're distracted by our responsibilities and routines, the bustle of others around us, a constant barrage of information and entertainment, and our own thoughts. It's also plain hard work to enter into God's presence through prayer, especially when we haven't made it a habit.

How can we make it a habit? Through sufficient motivation and consistent practice.

Keith Phillips

> Then He said, "Go out, and stand on the mountain before the LORD." And behold, the LORD passed by, and a great and strong wind tore into the mountains and broke the rocks in pieces before the LORD, but the LORD was not in the wind; and after the wind an earthquake, but the LORD was not in the earthquake; and after the earthquake a fire, but the LORD was not in the fire; and after the fire a still small voice.
>
> *1 Kings 19:11–12* ∎

---

[1] 2 Corinthians 3:18

The people who
accomplish the most
do so not because they
never run into problems,
but because they believe
there is a solution for
every one.
Maria Fontaine

Never let yesterday
use up too much
of today.
Will Rogers

Reboot

A SPIRITUAL EXERCISE

THE APOSTLES, WHEN THEY HAD RETURNED, TOLD HIM ALL
THAT THEY HAD DONE. THEN HE TOOK THEM AND WENT ASIDE
PRIVATELY INTO A DESERTED PLACE.

Luke 9:10

It's a typical busy day, filled with the usual responsibilities at home and work, but then more than the usual number of unexpected things come up. You manage to keep going, but notice that you're running slower, losing focus, and feeling overwhelmed.

What's one of the first things most people try when their computer starts running slower or having other problems? They save their work and reboot their computer, which clears the computer's cluttered memory. Often that is exactly what was needed to get the computer working efficiently again.

When you see that it's taking you longer than it should to complete the task at hand, it may seem like a waste of precious time to stop long enough to clear your mind and settle your spirit, but you'll probably waste more time and energy in the long run if you don't. You would be like the person whose computer is running slow or acting up, but who doesn't want to take the time to clear the computer's overloaded memory by rebooting.

Here are a few things that you can do to "reboot" yourself, all of which involve stepping back from your work for a few minutes: Take a short walk in the fresh air. Take a few deep breaths to clear your lungs. Stretch. Do some light exercises to get your heart rate up a little. Look out the window at God's creation. Count your blessings. Enjoy a cup of tea. Take a short nap.

Before you go back to work, ask Jesus to put each of the tasks still ahead of you in perspective. Reassess your priorities and adjust your work plan accordingly.

Abi May ■

The kingfisher effect

JESUS ANSWERED AND SAID TO THEM, "HAVE FAITH IN GOD."
Mark 11:22

When Japan's Sanyo Shinkansen "bullet train" was first put in service, residents along the train line complained about the noise level. About half the line was made up of tunnel sections, and the train would produce a tunnel boom on exiting due to the sudden change in air resistance.

The engineers pondered the problem until one of them remembered having read about a bird with a unique design feature, the kingfisher. To catch its prey, the kingfisher dives from the air, which has low resistance, into high-resistance water—and it only creates the smallest splash upon entry. The engineer surmised that this was due to the shape of the kingfisher's beak being perfectly suited to deal with such changes in resistance.

He and his colleagues conducted simulations by shooting various shapes into a pipe and measuring the pressure waves on exit. The data showed that the ideal shape for the nose of the bullet train was almost identical to a kingfisher's beak—problem solved! The engineers probably would have had a much more difficult time finding the solution if they had relied solely on their training and experience as mechanical engineers. The solution was found only when one of them looked elsewhere.

One of the problems with problems is that we tend to rely too much on our own abilities and experience to solve them, when God often has a better idea. It takes faith to stop trying so hard on our own and turn to God for help, but that's usually what it takes for Him to get through to us. Faith is to problems what the kingfisher's beak is to water. When obstacles present themselves, the sudden added resistance to our plans or routine can give us quite a jolt, but faith helps us find solutions quicker and with less wear and tear on our nerves. Faith doesn't eliminate all our problems, but it lessens their impact.

David Bolick ■

Slowdown or meltdown

*That you may walk worthy of the Lord, fully pleasing
Him, being fruitful in every good work and
increasing in the knowledge of God.*
Colossians 1:10

Wouldn't it be better to recognize your limits, slow it down,
just do so much and no more, and leave the rest until later? Even
though you wouldn't get as much done as you previously thought
you needed to, you would still accomplish quite a bit, while staying
healthy and happy. That's certainly better than trying to do too
much and cracking up! Sooner or later, one way or the other, you'll
have to slow down—either because you wisely choose to, or because
you're forced to.

We tend to think we're stronger and more capable and more
indispensable than we are. And if we carry on in that frame of
mind, trying to do everything ourselves, we just might find out
how dispensable we are. When we collapse physically, mentally, or
emotionally and can't get anything done, we'll find out that the
world can go on without us.

Sometimes God has to dispel our delusions of grandeur, our feelings of self-importance. He knows we have our limits, and He knows how frail we are. "He knows our frame; He remembers that we are dust."[1] He just wishes that we would wake up and realize that too.

The solution is to slow down and go at a slower daily pace.

In today's fast-paced world it's very difficult to slow down due to the many demands on our time, but finding that balance is something we should be doing constantly, because moderation in all things is one of the keys to physical health and spiritual well-being.

Maria Fontaine ∎

[1] Psalm 103:14

Finding time for prayer

It takes time to communicate with anyone, including God. There's no way around it. It's a mistake, though, to think of time spent in prayer as time that could have been better used to get other things done, because if you take time to pray, you'll be able to get a lot more done than you would otherwise. It's an investment, but once you start reaping the benefits, you'll wonder how you ever managed without it. Here are a few tips to help get you started:

Make a conscious effort. Like forming any new habit, this will take consistent determination. In time, though, you'll find that you're remembering to pray more, and forgetting to less.

Make prayer a priority. You always have time for the things you consider most important.

Set aside specific times in your daily routine. If you wait till everything else is taken care of, it will never happen. If you find that one time of day doesn't work well for you, try another. If you miss your appointed times one day, don't give up! Try again the next day.

Set attainable goals. It's not how long you pray that counts, but how earnest and sincere you are and how much you believe your prayers will be answered.

Take advantage of spare moments. You can pray during a coffee break, when stuck in traffic, while waiting for an appointment, while cooking, while taking a shower, while waiting for the baby to drift off to sleep, while walking the dog—almost any time, really.

Pray before starting each new task. "In all your ways acknowledge [God], and He shall direct your paths."[1] In many cases, a prayer of only a sentence or two is all it takes.

Pray at the first sign of trouble. Ask for clarity of thought, composure, strength, inspiration, or answers—whatever you need at the moment—and God will give it.[2]

Alex Peterson ∎

[1] Proverbs 3:6

[2] Matthew 7:7

Let Me help

THE PEACE OF GOD, WHICH SURPASSES ALL UNDERSTANDING,
WILL GUARD YOUR HEARTS AND MINDS
THROUGH CHRIST JESUS.
Philippians 4:7

Life wasn't designed to coast through without any troubles or hardships. There will always be setbacks, difficulties, and pressures, but if you learn to see those as challenges that I can help you overcome, I will do just that.

I want to lift the weight of uncertainty from your shoulders. I want you to hold on to the knowledge that no matter how great the need, how dark the night, or how seemingly impossible the situation, I am in control and never fail those who turn to Me for help. No matter what you are up against, you and I can overcome it. Allow Me to work on your behalf.

When you find yourself in a stressful situation and decide to trust Me to bring you through it, your faith releases My power, which is vastly greater than your own. You may be able to sort things out eventually, but I can help you do it much quicker. You may be able to withstand a lot of pressure, but I can relieve the pressure. You may be able to do something well, but you and I can do it better.

I will never leave your side. I will make good on My promises to move mountains,[1] give you sustaining grace,[2] rest of spirit,[3] and peace that surpasses understanding.[4] No matter what is going on around you, you can be at peace when you are anchored deeply in Me. Beneath the churning waves, your anchor will hold.

Come to Me, lay your burdens on My shoulders, and find that I have all you need.

A message from Jesus received in prayer ■

[1] Matthew 17:20

[2] 2 Corinthians 12:9

[3] Matthew 11:28

[4] Philippians 4:7

CHAPTER 12

Pioneering: Fresh Beginnings

THE STEPS OF A GOOD MAN ARE ORDERED BY THE LORD,
AND HE DELIGHTS IN HIS WAY.
Psalm 37:23

Build today, then, strong and sure,
With a firm and ample base;
And ascending and secure
Shall tomorrow find its place.
Henry Wadsworth Longfellow

Seize the day!

This is the day the Lord has made;
We will rejoice and be glad in it.
Psalm 118:24

One of the most tragic things I know about human nature
is that all of us tend to put off living. We are all dreaming of
some magical rose garden over the horizon instead of enjoying
the roses that are blooming outside our windows today.
Dale Carnegie

What is not started today is never finished tomorrow.
Johann Wolfgang von Goethe

You had better live your best and act your best and think your
best today; for today is the sure preparation for tomorrow
and all the other tomorrows that follow.
Harriet Martineau

Light tomorrow with today!
Elizabeth Barrett Browning

A fresh mind keeps the body fresh. Take in the ideas of the
day, drain off those of yesterday. As to the morrow, time
enough to consider it when it becomes today.
Edward George Bulwer-Lytton ■

A new morning, a fresh start

A SPIRITUAL EXERCISE

MORNING BY MORNING NEW MERCIES I SEE!
GREAT IS THY FAITHFULNESS DEAR LORD UNTO ME.
Thomas Chisholm

Every morning is a new chance to do things differently, better than we have before—especially when we take time to connect with God, get His perspective on the areas we want to improve in, and ask Him to help us make the necessary adjustments in our thinking, attitudes, and actions. In fact, there is nothing He would rather do than help us change for the better.

A wonderful way to start your day is with a prayer of thanksgiving to God for His loving care. Take a few minutes first thing tomorrow morning to do this, and see what a difference it makes in your day. You can use the following prayer, or one of your own. Or start with this one, and tailor it to your circumstances by adding specifics.

Thank You for this new day, fresh and clean, unspoiled by yesterday's messes and mistakes. While I was sleeping, You cleaned them all up and made all things new.

Thank You for brand-new mercy, brand-new love, brand-new forgiveness, renewed strength, and Your unfailing promise of help. You're so wonderful to me, so patient with my shortcomings and my weaknesses. You don't look at my faults or condemn me for my mistakes, but always offer me hope.

I leave all my mistakes and failures behind. Help me to go forward, with my hand in Yours.

Abi May

My voice You shall hear in the morning, O LORD;
In the morning I will direct it to You,
And I will look up.
Psalm 5:3 ■

Crossroads

YOUR EARS SHALL HEAR A WORD BEHIND YOU, SAYING,
"THIS IS THE WAY, WALK IN IT,"
WHENEVER YOU TURN TO THE RIGHT HAND
OR WHENEVER YOU TURN TO THE LEFT.
Isaiah 30:21

Crossroads are a wonderful place to be because you have so many options. You can go forward, return the way you came, or go in a new direction, either to the right or to the left.

Crossroads aren't always welcome, though, because they force people to make decisions, and that can be an uncomfortable process. Especially in the case of major or potentially life-changing decisions, no one really likes the hard work of thinking and praying the matter through, the soul-searching involved.

I use the crossroads of life to help some people come to terms with mistakes or wrong turns they've made, and to give them a chance to get going in the right direction. For others who haven't been off track, it's a chance to go in a new direction that will make them even happier and get them farther in the long run. For yet others, it's a time to confirm that they're going in the right direction, so they can continue with the vigor that renewed conviction brings. Whatever the case, whenever someone comes to a crossroads, it's an opportunity, because if they ask Me which way they should go, I'll show them.

You can't fail as long as you're looking to Me and are open to whatever road I have for you. Maybe it will be something you've never done before. It might even be something you're afraid to do. Or it could be the same thing that you've done for years. Whichever road I ask you to take I will also equip you for, even if you don't think you have what it will take right now. As you take a step in the direction I'm leading you, I'll give you what it takes. If you need more faith, I'll give you more faith. If you need more courage, I'll give you more courage. If you need more love, I'll give you more love. If you need more strength or perseverance, I'll give you those things. Step by step, as you follow Me, I will continue to do that. Whatever you need for your journey, I'll give you that.

So instead of being afraid of those crossroad signs, you can look forward to them with anticipation, knowing that I'm by your side to instruct you and guide you and help you. I know your heart, and I know where you will be happiest and most fulfilled. If you don't know where that is, just ask Me to point you in the right direction and start walking. I am always with you, no matter where you are and what you're doing. I'm right beside you each step of the way. As you learn to hear My voice in your mind, pointing the way, you'll really make progress. I love you, and I'll never fail you.

A message from Jesus received in prayer ∎

Obstacles cannot crush
me. Every obstacle
yields to stern resolve.
He who is fixed to a
star does not change
his mind.
Leonardo da Vinci

Do something for
somebody every
day for which you
do not get paid.
Albert Schweitzer

A prayer for times of change

THE WAYS OF RIGHT-LIVING PEOPLE GLOW WITH LIGHT; THE
LONGER THEY LIVE, THE BRIGHTER THEY SHINE.
Proverbs 4:18 (THE MESSAGE)

Heavenly Father, Your creation is changing continually—seasons and cycles in perpetual motion. Help me to flow like that, to not be afraid to let go of my comfortable habits and routines in order to discover new things. Instead of holing up in the security of the familiar, help me to venture out into new territory. Help me to not stagnate, but to progress and continue to grow. Most of all, help me to change in the ways You want me to change, so I can become all You know I can be. ∎

Few events capture the world's attention like the World Cup does every four years. For instance, the 2006 final attracted an estimated television audience of 715 million, and the entire process, including qualifying and elimination rounds, a total of over 26 billion—the equivalent of nearly four views for every person in the world. Even those who normally pay little or no attention to sports are drawn in when Cup results are front-page news.

For us spectators, depending on how closely we follow football (soccer) and how well our team does, the buildup may last a year, the final match a couple of hours, and the celebration a few days. Then we return to our normal lives. But for players, coaches, and others involved at the highest level, the World Cup is a defining moment, the culmination of years of dreaming, planning, sacrificing, and hard work.

It's a defining moment, but it's not the be-all and end-all of their lives, as it must have seemed when they were entirely focused on making it to the World Cup and doing well there. It's really just a milestone, a new beginning. The real tests start now. How will the losers take defeat? Will they give up, or press on and possibly win next time? What opportunities will open for the winners, and how will they handle success? Will they use it to further their football fortunes, or to secure other careers after football, or to promote causes that are important to them? In the months and years to come we'll find out who those big names really are.

And it's much the same for us. We may not be athletes in the world spotlight, but every day is another chance to examine who we really are and decide what we want to be known and remembered for. Every day can be a defining moment, if we make it so.

Keith Phillips ■

CHAPTER 13

Progress: Forward Motion

AS YOUR DAYS, SO SHALL YOUR STRENGTH BE.

Deuteronomy 33:25

A family had a few apple trees at the bottom of their garden. The trees yielded more fruit than could be eaten immediately or given to neighbors, so some needed to be stored for the coming months.

One fall, little Tommy was finally big enough to help his mother store the apples. They had been picked and piled up in a basket with care, as bruised apples will spoil. Now it was time to transfer them to storage racks in the cellar.

Tommy, eager to help, put his arms around a dozen shiny apples and tried to carry them over to the rack. To his dismay, one by one the apples dropped out of his arms until they were all on the floor.

His mother wasn't too worried. "Here, let me show you," she said gently as she put his hands around one apple. "Take this one and put it over there, and then come back and get another one."

Too often we try to put our arms around a year or a month or a week, but God tells us, "Take it a day at a time."[1] We aren't equipped to carry all of our future cares at once, but we can if we face each challenge as it comes.

Abi May

Expect great things from God.
Attempt great things for God.
William Carey ∎

[1] See Matthew 6:34

God at the wheel

I can still remember when it was just me—self-assured, confident, and proud of my ability to maneuver my car along life's road. I was master of my fate. I loved those solitary hours on the highway, watching the sun sink below the horizon. I loved the feel of the wheels gripping the road. I loved being able to go anywhere at a whim, wherever my fancy would take me at the moment. Life was all mine to enjoy, and I did my best to live it up.

Sure, there were hard times too—lonely, dark stretches of road in the night that seemed to almost swallow me up, times when I had to lie flat on my back in the mud, trying to find a mechanical problem or stop an oil leak, times when I had to replace a blown tire in scorching sun or pouring rain, moments of confusion and frustration attempting to reverse out of dead ends. No, being alone wasn't all fun and games, but I always managed to brush off those unfortunate incidents and set out again in search of new adventures.

Then one day You hitched a ride. When I asked where You were going, You said, "Wherever you're going," and I soon discovered a wonderful friendship. You were always there to hold the map and to give directions when I was lost. Somehow all the routes were known to You. You were there too in the darkness of those long night drives, to hold my hand when I was afraid and lonely. Somehow Your presence always made the darkness bright.

You were there to push when I needed to get back onto the road after my quest for adventure would land me in a ditch. Somehow You understood my disappointment, and You never said, "I told you so." You were even there to embrace and forgive after I foolishly argued with You and told You to get out of my life. Somehow You kept loving me and having faith in me. But still I insisted on driving. "After all, it's my car," I would remind You. And although I was thankful for Your advice and directions, the final decision always rested with me. "After all, it's my life."

Miles and miles flew by, and still I insisted on remaining in the driver's seat, ignoring Your offers to take control—that is, until the day I totaled my car. Humiliated and heartbroken, my dream car in pieces, I finally handed You the car keys. With a smile of relief, You rolled up Your sleeves and went to work making repairs. In no time we were back on the road, with You as the driver and me as the passenger.

Relinquishing control was far more difficult than I had expected. "Hey!" I would yell, lunging at the steering wheel. "What are You doing? I thought we'd agreed to go that way!" Immediately You would brake and patiently wait until I had stopped struggling to regain control. Then You would turn to me and say with all the tenderness of a father explaining to his child, "Trust Me. I know what I am doing." Reluctantly I would surrender and sit, chafing in my seat until we turned the next corner. Suddenly it would become abundantly clear that You did know where You were taking me, and I would turn to You with a look of amazement at Your wisdom and foresight.

But that was a lesson I would soon forget, and before long I'd be at it again. We would pass an amusement, and I would whine, "Hey, why didn't You stop?" You would smile knowingly and say, "Trust Me. I have something far better up ahead." And sure enough, there was always something far better.

After a while I grew accustomed to Your driving. I learned to sit on my hands and bite my tongue when Your ways ran contrary to mine, forcing myself to patiently wait until the next bend in the road revealed the surprise behind that mysterious smile of Yours. Blowouts and wrong turns became a thing of the past too, as were my frantic searches for happiness and excitement. There never seemed to be a dull moment with You in the driver's seat.

That's not to say there weren't momentary disappointments, like the times You turned down lonely, dusty roads, and it was just the two of us for miles. But those lonely routes led to some of the most breathtaking views, panoramas full of hidden, mysterious beauty that You had reserved for us alone. There were also times when You chose routes that led through places I had always dreaded—dark, sunless valleys and canyons. Why here? I would silently protest—but You could always tell what I was thinking and would ask, "Have I ever failed you before?" As I forced my soul to be still and trust, I found strength and courage that I had not known I had.

Since the day that You took the wheel, I've been taken to breathtaking heights and to valleys with a beauty all their own; I've experienced the thrill of adventure, incredible happiness, and love without measure. You were right. I would never regret a life spent with You at the wheel.

Christina Andreassen ∎

Three things you can do to make the most of your day

ASK OF ME.
Psalm 2:8

Number one, talk to Me first thing or even the night before about what you need or want to do. It doesn't have to take long—just long enough to get your bearings on the day and to let Me remind you of anything you may have forgotten.

Number two, each time you are about to start a new task, ask Me if you're on the right track. It may seem like the logical thing to do, or you may have done it a thousand times before, but perhaps I see factors you don't see or want to show you a better way to do it. When you make a conscious effort to check your plans with Me, it's much easier for Me to help you get it right. Nothing is too small to ask Me about.

Number three, when new factors arise, ask Me what to do. I see the big picture, and I can help you see things more clearly too. The quickest and surest route isn't always a straight line. Sometimes you need to sidestep or even backtrack. I know the way, but I can only lead you step by step if you ask Me step by step.

If you will remember to do these three things, your days will go better and you will have the peace of mind that comes from knowing that you made the most of your day. As you get in the habit of involving Me in your plans and work, you will also come to know Me in a deeper, more personal way. Each day will take on a new dimension—the dimension of My loving, guiding presence.

A message from Jesus received in prayer ■

Secrets of their success

Ask those who have achieved greatness in any field for the secrets of their success, and somewhere near the top of most lists will be a visualization of their goal. Throughout years of rigorous training, the Olympic champion pictured himself on the podium, receiving his gold medal. The prima ballerina saw herself doing grand jetés on the world's finest stages. The Nobel-winning scientist imagined his eureka moment. The star saleswoman mentally packed her bags 365 times for that prize spa vacation. It took hard work to be sure, but they got where they did in part by picturing themselves already there. When it finally happened, many will tell you, it was exactly as they had seen it in their mind's eye.

Read the Bible's "Faith Hall of Fame" chapter, Hebrews 11, and you'll see that this visualization technique is nothing new. It says of Noah, Abraham, Moses, and others who did extraordinary things,

"These all died in faith, not having received the promises, but having seen them afar off were assured of them."[1] Like the Olympian, the ballerina, the Nobel laureate, and the saleswoman, they each focused on the prize, but with one important difference. The things for which these Bible greats are most remembered were merely steppingstones to the ultimate prize they strove for—God's eternal reward for a life that was pleasing to Him.

So if you want to succeed, "keep your eye on the prize"—whatever it is that you want to get out of life. And for the ultimate in success, find out what God wants you to contribute in this life. Only He knows that, but He will tell you if you ask. Set your sights on that, and God will not only give you the extra umph you need, He will heap on blessings all along the way. And when this life is over, you'll hear Him say, "Well done!"[2] What could be better than that?

Keith Phillips ■

[1] Hebrews 11:13

[2] Matthew 25:23

Afterword

Visualize a mountain range. Focus on a picture, or use your imagination. Tag each peak as one of the challenges in your life—an area where you want to succeed or where you're facing a problem. Have you worried as these difficulties loomed large on your horizon? It's time for a change in your perspective!

Choose one of the peaks and picture yourself climbing it. It's somewhat of a struggle getting up the rocky slopes, but you are not climbing alone. A strong, experienced, and capable mountain guide accompanies you. The Lord promises, "I will instruct you and teach you in the way you should go; I will guide you."[1] He offers a helping hand as you clamber over rocks. He guides you in a safe path. Together you can make this climb. You're cheerful, even eager, as you anticipate reaching the summit. Remember, this is an exciting challenge, not a drudgery. Now, picture you and Jesus celebrating together at the summit. You've reached your goal!

Abi May ∎

[1] Psalm 32:8

OTHER TITLES IN THIS SERIES

Quiet Moments for Parents

Quiet Moments When You Need Them Most

Quiet Moments for Busy Days

ABOUT THE COMPILER

Abi May is a British educator and member of the Institute for Learning.
She is also a writer and compiler who specializes in inspirational anthologies.
Previous books include:

The Wonder of Christmas (2007, Aurora Production)
The Wonder of Love (2011, Aurora Production)
The Wonder of Mothers (2011, Aurora Production)
The Wonder of Fathers (2011, Aurora Production)
Moments in Morning (2012, Aurora Production)